Complexity in Economics
Emerging macro behaviour from micro interactions

Eniel Ninka

Contents

List of Figures

List of Tables

0
Acknowledgements

This book is based on my Doctoral Thesis. Therefore, there are many people that I would like to thank for having contributed in some manner to its realization.

First of all I would like to thank two of my colleagues of the Doctoral Course: Raffaella Santolini, for her constant support, and Saul Desiderio, for his advice on code writing and modelling.

There are several individuals at the Department of Economics of Ancona, Italy that I would like to thank. Firstly, Professor Mauro Gallegati, my thesis supervisor, who introduced me to the world of Complexity in Economics. Secondly, Professor Fabio Fiorillo, discussant of the thesis, for having read and commented on the manuscript. Thirdly, Professors Alberto Zazzaro, Paolo Pettenati and Giuseppe Cannullo with whom I collaborated as a teaching assistant. Then, professors Riccardo 'Jack' Lucchetti and Piero Alessandrini whose friendship and words made me be a wiser man. Last, but not least, I really wish to thank Giulio 'Bomber' Palomba for several reasons: for having been always prompt to help me whenever I had problems with LaTeX or Econometrics, and for his very useful and brilliant comments.

I feel heavily indebted to Dr. Simone Landini and to Dr. Alberto Russo for their invaluable help in programming and code debugging. Moreover, I am grateful to Simone for having contributed with ideas during the modelling phase.

At the end, I would like to express my deepest love to my parents.

They have supported me constantly during my permanence in Italy. This book is dedicated to them.

The responsibility for all the errors and other flaws is obviously entirely mine.

1
Introduction

"I think the next century will be the century of complexity."
Stephen Hawking

The XX century Traditional Economics has been dominated by the Neoclassical paradigm. Its foundational notions are rational, optimizing consumers and producers making choices in a world of finite resources. This combination of self-interest and constraints then drives the economy to the Pareto optimal point of equilibrium. The methodology of economic analysis has also been dominated by the use of mathematical proofs which begin with a set of assumptions and then build logically up to a set of conclusions.

In this book we depart from the General Equilibrium theory with its godlike Walrasian Auctioneer and fully rational and perfectly foresighted agents. We build an evolving network of fully decentralized trades among bounded rational, adaptive agents, where explanations are not derived deductively, but generated from the analysis of interactions. The aim of this work is to build a model which, through simple rules of behaviour of agents at an individual level, manages to produce some empirical regularities at a micro and at a macro level. Such a model could be used in the future as a computational laboratory for conducting policy experiments.

Plan of the work

In Chapter 2 we give an overview of the two main approaches to the economic science. On the one hand, there is what is generally called the Traditional or Neoclassical Approach. This is the mainstream approach in Economics and it has dominated the scene for over one century. It builds on the mechanistic and reductionist view of the science. It makes use of mathematical tools on the study of the economic phenomena. The reductionist approach is materialized in the use of the representative agent, since all agents are considered to be homogeneous. The use of the representative agent in economics have been criticized, among others, by Alan Kirman (1992). Kirman's vision is to consider the economy as a complex system in which the interactions of a multitude of heterogeneous agents at a micro level generates the emergence of phenomena at a macro level (emerging macroeconomics).

On the other hand, there is the Agent-Based Modelling approach. Agent-based modelling is a useful and powerful tool in modelling the economy as a complex system (Tesfatsion, 2002, 2003, 2005). The economic system is considered as an open system and, in particular, as a Complex Adaptive System. ABM builds on the use of computer simulations to solve models composed of many non-linear interactions and equations (consequently difficult to solve analytically). In these models agents are heterogeneous, their interaction happens at an individual level and there are positive and negative feedbacks. Such virtual worlds are particularly powerful, flexible and useful for conducting policy experiments, perfect laboratories for testing, in a controlled situation, conjectures and various hypothesis on the economic system. This branch of Economics is called Agent-Based Computational Economics (ACE).

In Chapter 3 we describe a model of a simplified economy with heterogeneous interacting agents. Even though agents do not optimize their outcome and are not characterized by fully rational behaviour, but more realistically try to reach *satisficing* results, complex phenomena at a macro level emerge as a consequence of agents' interaction at the individual level.

In Chapter 4 we review several stylized facts at micro and macro level. Then we compare the model generated data with empirical evidence, in order to check the soundness of our model's microfoundations. We firstly discuss a simplified version of the model. Then, we go a step further and introduce new features to our model.

Finally, in Chapter 5 we make some conclusive considerations and propose an agenda for future research.

1.Introduction

2

From the Classics to CATS Models. A Short Story

"Economists set themselves too easy, too useless a task
if in tempestuous seasons they can only tell us that
when the storm is long past the ocean is flat again."
John Maynard Keynes[1]

2.1 Introduction

Over the past decade there has been a surge in criticism of economic theory. In a controversial article titled "The decline of Economics" the author, John Cassidy , charged that economics had disappeared into an ivory-tower world of highly idealized theory, untested by data, and packed with unrealistic assumptions. He claimed that economics had become a "giant academic game" in which economists wrote papers for each other, showing off their mathematical brilliance, but demonstrating little interest in the relevance of their theories to the real world data (Cassidy, 1996). In the same article Cassidy quoted Joseph Stiglitz saying "Anybody looking at these models would say they can't provide a good description of the modern world". The Traditional approach to economics has shaped the way the economic science has been done during the past century. Without doubt, eco-

---

[1]Keynes (1923)

17

nomics has produced some enormously powerful and influential ideas, ranging from the efficiency of markets to the benefits of free trade and the importance of individual choice. The use of interest rates to manage inflation, monetary and fiscal policies to dampen the business cycle, encouragement of competition, environmental and labour regulations to protect people from the failures of the market etc. are all ideas that have been developed during the last century. Nevertheless, the too unrealistic assumptions of the formal theories and mathematical models and the contradictions between their results and the real-world data has called for a new and a better way of doing science in economics. In this chapter we will, very briefly, present some of the characterizing features of what is better known as the Neoclassical approach (Section 2.2). We will pass then onto discussing the Complexity approach to economics which considers the economic system as a Complex Adaptive System and adopts to its study methods proper to the study of the complex systems (Section 2.3). The Agent-based Modelling offers new theoretical ways of exploring such complex adaptive social systems (Section 2.4). Finally, we will discuss some Agent-Based Models, and in particular the CATS Models, in Section 2.5.

2.2 The Neoclassical Approach

There are two fundamental questions that the economic science has tried to answer throughout its history: how wealth is created and how wealth is allocated[2]. Both questions were extensively addressed by Adam Smith in "The Wealth of Nations". His answer to the first question was simple but powerful: economic value is created when people take raw materials from their environment and then, through their labour, turn those materials into something that people want. Smith's great insight was that the secret to wealth creation was improving the productivity of labour. In turn, the secret to greater

---

[2]The analysis presented in this section owes much to the work of Beinhocker (2006)

productivity was the division of labour and the specialization that it enables, that Smith explained citing the famous example of the pin factory. In other words, Smith recognized that only the specialization would permit a growth of the wealth of a nation on a per-capita basis.

The other question that Smith addressed was not just how wealth and the resources are allocated in a society, but how they should be allocated, i.e. what is the fair allocation for both the individual and the society as a whole. In Smith's view, the most just mechanism for allocating resources from the point of view of the individual was the one that enabled people to pursue their own self-interest and make their own choices. At the same time, the best allocation of resources for society as a whole was the one that put resources to their most efficient use, thus maximizing the total wealth of the society. Smith's view on how this objective should be achieved was radical: competitive markets are the most morally just mechanism for allocating a society's resources. Smith argued that if people were left to trade freely, self-interest would drive them to provide the goods and services people need. *"It is not from the benevolence of the butcher, the brewer, or the baker, that we expect our dinner, but from their regard to their own interest. We address ourselves, not to their humanity but to their self-love, and never talk to them of our own necessities but of their advantages."* (Smith (1776), Book I, Ch. II.[3]). Furthermore, the combination of competition and the profit motive would drive these people to provide their goods and services as efficiently as possible. *"Every individual is continually exerting himself to find out the most advantageous employment for whatever capital he can command."* (Smith (1776), Book IV, Ch. II.[4]). According to Smith, this pursuit of self-interest would in turn benefit the society as a whole: *"[The merchant] generally, indeed, neither intends to promote the public interest, nor knows how much he is promoting it....[H]e intends only his own gain, and he is in this, as in many other cases, led by*

---

[3]Of the Principle which gives occasion to the Division of Labour

[4]Of Restraints upon the Importation from Foreign Countries of such Goods as can be produced at Home

an invisible hand to promote an end which was no part of his intention....By pursuing his own interest he frequently promotes that of the society more effectually than when he really intends to promote it" (Smith (1776), ibidem). The *"invisible hand"* that would lead to the efficient allocation of resources was the mechanism of competitive markets and the price provides the key mechanism through which producers and consumers meet in the marketplace. Left to their own, without any kind of restrictions, the combination of self-interest and competitive markets would naturally bring the economy to a point of balance.

While Smith described the role of markets in achieving the balance between supply and demand, he did not describe in detail the decision-making process by which self-interested producers determine how much product to supply, or how self-interested consumers determine how much to demand. The main contributions on this would come from Jacques Turgout and Jeremy Bentham .

On the basis of his observations on the work of farmers, Turgot articulated what has come to be known as the law of diminishing returns. It proved to be a crucial concept because it linked producers costs in the supply side of supply and demand. Another important contribution, this time on the demand side, was made by Bentham. Smith had identified human self-interest as the motivating force driving the economy, but did not explain how that self-interest translated into specific economic decisions. Bentham argued that the pursuit of self-interest was a rational activity based on a calculus of pleasure and pain. He identified a quantity that he called *utility* to measure individual pleasure and pain. Therefore, economic choices were the result of an individual's calculations as to what actions would maximize the proper utility.

Years later, the German economist Hermann Gossen built on Bentham's ideas and articulated what we know as the law of diminishing marginal utility. This law was in essence the flip side of the Turgot's law. Just as Turgot showed that there were diminishing benefits to increased production, Gossen showed that there were also diminishing benefits to increased consumption. The combination of diminishing marginal returns on production and diminishing marginal utility on consumption means that markets have a natural balancing mechanism – price. Price is the information the producers and consumers share. A price increase will simultaneously lower the consumption and raise the production, while a price decrease will do the reverse.

The classical economics was not a mathematical field. In fact, earlier economists like Smith regarded themselves as philosophers rather than scientists. It was not until Leon Walras completed his masterwork, "Elements of a Pure Economics", in 1872 (Backhouse, 2002). Walras radically changed the way economics was being done. The XIX century was an era of great scientific progress. Following Newton's great discoveries in the XVII century, a series of scientists and mathematicians, including Leibniz, Lagrange, Euler, and Hamilton, developed new mathematical tools, like the differential equations, to deal with a wide range of natural phenomena. The success of these theories gave scientists a boundless optimism that they could describe any aspect of nature in their equations (Stewart, 1989). Walras was convinced that if the equations of the differential calculus could capture the motions of atoms and planets in the universe, they could also capture the motion of human minds in the economy. What Walras saw was a parallel between the idea of balancing points in economic systems and balancing points, or equilibrium points, in nature (Ingrao and Israel, 1990). One of Walras's objectives in bringing mathematics to economics was to make economic systems predictable. Since unstable equilibriums are hard to predict (if not impossible) and so do are systems with multiple equilibrium points, it became clear to Walras that what he needed was a single, stable equilibrium point. He assumed that for each commodity traded in a market, there was only one price, one equilibrium point, at which traders would be satisfied and the market would clear. The supply and the demand were the two balance forces in the system and therefore prices would in a predictable way settle to their equilibrium level. Walras imported the concept of equilibrium from physics into economics and laid the foundations of the Traditional Economics (Ingrao and Israel, 1990). In building his equilibrium model, Walras considered as given the production side of the economy and focused on trading between consumers. He assumed that various goods already exist in the economy and the problem is to determine how prices are set and how the goods would be allocated among the individuals involved. Walras assumed that each person was initially endowed with a random sampling of all the goods available in the economy and that trading would then move the economy from the initial random, out-of-equilibrium state into the equilibrium state. To make the trading more organized and mathematically simpler, Walras imagined that the economy had an auctioneer and that one of the goods would be used as money. He called the auction process as *tâtonnement* and the final state as the general equilibrium point. Walras's use of sophisticated mathematics borrowed from physics was a real revolution for the economics. If one accepted Walras's assumptions that people had different utilities, and that they were rational and self-interested in maximizing those utilities, then one could predict with mathematical precision how they would trade and the relative prices that would be set in the economy. Issues such as the existence of the auctioneer and the observation and measurement of individual utilities were considered as details to be addressed in the future, a small price to pay for the ability to make mathematically precise, scientific predictions about things like prices in the economy for the first time (Mirovski, 1989). Walras's willingness to make trade-offs in realism for the sake of mathematical predictability would set a pattern followed by economists over the next century.

William Jevons was a contemporary of Walras, and like Walras, Jevons was an eager reader of physics books in search of inspiration. He was fascinated by new theories developed by Faraday and Maxwell for describing gravity, magnetism and electricity as "fields of force", and, as Walras had done, he imported the concepts into economics. In Jevon's conception, self-interest provides the force, like gravity, that pulls us to maximize our utility. But, since we live in a world of finite resources which provides the constraints to our action, we should find the combination of goods and services that maximizes our utility within such constraints. As in Walras's model, we use trade to get to this state. Jevon's main contribution was to portray the problem of economic choice as an exercise in constrained optimization.

Vilfredo Pareto gave a further contribution. He demonstrated that since it takes two consenting people to trade and people are not stupid, they would only engage in trades that were either win-win trades or at least win-no-lose, both of which would eventually raise the total welfare of the participants. Therefore, people would continue to trade until they do not reach the equilibrium point, later called Pareto Optimal, i.e. the point at which no further trades can be made without making someone worse-off.

To sum up, according to the theories of Smith, Walras, Jevons and Pareto (and naturally of other economists, whom we now call), in a market economy people freely trade and they eventually reach a state where they are as satisfied as possible, given the resources available. By the means of such trading, the economy reaches an equilibrium, a natural resting point, where supply equals demand, where resources are put to their most efficient use, and where the welfare of society is Pareto Optimal.

Marginalists laid the foundations of the economic science. In the XX century a series of economists, including Alfred Marshall, John Hicks, Paul Samuelson, Joseph Schumpeter, Kenneth Arrow, Gérard Debreu, John Maynard Keynes, , Robert Solow, Milton Friedman, Robert Lucas, and many others, consolidated and built on those foundations.

Marshall connected Jevon's model of a single market in isolation (partial equilibrium) with Walras's model of many interlinked markets in an economy (general equilibrium). Hicks synthesized the work of Walras, Pareto and Marshall into a coherent theory in his "Value and Capital". Samuelson gave very important contributions to the theory of consumer behaviour in Traditional Economics. Arrow and Debreu connected Walras's notion of general equilibrium with Pareto's concept of optimality in a very general way, thus creating the Neoclassical theory of general equilibrium. Their theorem showed that all the markets in the economy together would automatically coordinate on a set of prices that was Pareto optimal for the economy as a whole and that this would occur even when there is uncertainty in the market (Mas-Colell *et al.*, 1995). This automatic coordination occurs because markets are linked together by the ability of some goods to act as substitutes for others and other goods to be complementary. Prices would transmit signals about supply and demand and self-interested people would react to those price signals driving the system to its socially optimal equilibrium.

What could be considered as the most interesting achievement of the Arrow-Debreu general equilibrium theory is that this important result was built up from a small set of axioms. Some of the assumptions were, nevertheless controversial and problematic. The theorem assumed that everyone is endowed with at least some amount of every commodity, that futures markets exist for every product and service, that everyone is extremely rational in calculating decisions, and knows the probabilities of all possible future states of the world. This assumptions were viewed as necessary simplifications. What was considered the very important thing was that one could start with a simple set of axioms and rigorously, mathematically build up to a very general result: rational self-interest operating in competitive markets would drive the economy to its optimal point.

Of the two fundamental questions that we mentioned in the beginning, the first one, how wealth is created, remained however without an answer until the mid XX century. The models of Walras , Jevons and so on, all began with the assumptions that an economy already exists, producers have resources, and consumers own various commodities. The problem was how to allocate the existing finite wealth of the economy in a way that provides the maximum benefit for everyone. An important reason for this focus on allocation of finite resources was that the mathematical equations of equilibrium imported from physics were ideal for answering the allocation question, but it was more difficult to apply them to growth. Equilibrium systems by definition are in a state of rest, while growth implies change and dynamism (Beinhocker, 2006).

Schumpeter was among the first economists to deal with the question of growth and innovation and the apparent contradiction between equilibrium and growth. The Neoclassical tended to view innovation as exogenous to the system, while Schumpeter believed that innovation had to be considered as endogenous to the economy an central to its understanding. He argued that a vital role in the economy is played by the figure of the entrepreneur. According to Schumpeter, technological progress occurred in a random stream of discoveries. However, new technologies would face numerous barriers to their commercialization, like the water behind a dam. In Schumpeter's theory, the entrepreneur played the role of the dam breaker, allowing a flood of innovation into the economy. In this way, growth comes to the economy not in a steady stream, but in "gales of creative destruction". Schumpeter, however, was never able to translate his theories into the rigorous language of mathematics. This was a shortcoming that limited their impact in Traditional Economics. Nevertheless, the Schumpeterian growth theories still have great appeal in the modern era economics (Beinhocker, 2006).

In 1956, in a landmark paper, Solow reconciled the equilibrium with the growth. He viewed the economy as being in a kind of dynamic equilibrium, or what he called balanced growth (Solow, 1956). Solow saw the economy as being balanced in equilibrium, even as it grew. He treated two key variables in the model as exogenous: the rate of population growth and the rate of technological change. These two variables drove the economic growth, and Solow showed that other factors in the economy, such as the rate of savings and the total amount of capital in the economy, would automatically be balanced in response to changes in population growth and technology. The Solow's model implied that only improvements in productivity could increase the per-capita wealth of a country and in his model the technology was key to productivity improvements.

By the end of the XX century, Traditional Economics was (quasi) entirely dominated by the Neoclassical paradigm with its foundational notions of rational, optimizing consumers and producers making choices in a world of finite resources. This combination of self-interest and constraints then drives the economy to the Pareto optimal point of equilibrium. The methodology of economic analysis was also dominated by the use of mathematical proofs that began with a set of assumptions and then built logically up to a set of conclusions.

The XX century economists had realized the ambition of creating a set of rigorous mathematical models for describing the workings of the economy. The Neoclassical growth theory claimed to answer the first great question of wealth creation, while the Neoclassical general equilibrium theory claimed to answer the second fundamental question of wealth allocation. Nonetheless, criticism on Traditional economic theory has been growing in the last decade.

Most Traditional Economics models begin with unrealistic assumptions and then, with mathematical inevitability, end up with equally unrealistic conclusions. This is why there is little empirical support or many core ideas of Traditional Economics, and in some cases empirical evidence directly contradicts theory's predictions.

To many critics, the assumptions of Traditional Economics do not appear as just simplifications of the reality, in order to be able to focus on a particular problem. A simplification must be done, but the model should be consistent with empirical evidence. Instead, it appears that beginning with Walras and Jevons, economists began arbitrarily making up assumptions about perfect rationality, godlike auctioneers, and so on with the sole purpose of making the equilibrium math work (Beinhocker, 2006). Some of the assumptions include lack of transaction costs, all products considered as pure commodities sold on price, firms working always as efficiently as possible, the possibility for consumers to purchase insurance for any possible eventuality, price being the only interaction mechanism, and so on.

Of all assumptions, perhaps the most obviously unrealistic one is the perfect rationality, i.e. people pursue their self-interest and achieve this by doing complex calculations. As Leijonhufvud put it, Traditional Economics model *"incredibly smart people in unbelievably simple situations"*, while the real world is more accurately described by *"believably simple people [dealing] with incredibly complex situations"* (Leijonhufvud, 1996). In fact, real people are quite poor at complex logical calculations. Instead, they engage in what Herbert Simon called *satisficing*, whereby one looks for a result that is good enough rather than the absolute best.

Another assumption of Traditional Economics is the dominance of negative feedbacks in the economic processes. A negative feedback is a decelerating, dampening, self-regulating cycle. Examples of negative feedback are the decreasing returns to production and consumption. Negative feedback keeps things contained, heading toward an equilibrium. The real word clearly does exhibit decreasing returns. But, as Arthur has argued, it also exhibits positive feedback (an accelerating, amplifying, self-reinforcing cycle), i.e. increasing returns (Arthur, 1994). For example, the more information becomes available on the Web, the more useful the Web becomes. Traditional Economics consider increasing-return phenomena as temporarily. It tends to assume a long run, in which all increasing returns have exhausted themselves and the economy can tun to equilibrium. Nevertheless, there is no long run in the real world. Quoting John Maynard Keynes, *"This long run is a misleading guide to current affairs. In the long run we are all dead. Economists set themselves too easy, too useless a task if in tempestuous seasons they can only tell us that when the storm is long past the ocean is flat again"*(Keynes, 1923, p. 65).

The physics of the Marginalists' period included the First Law of Thermodynamics, which states that the energy is neither created, nor destroyed, and is otherwise known as the Conservation of Energy Principle. One of the properties of this principle is that, if the total energy in a system is fixed (conserved), then the system will eventually reach the equilibrium. One of the consequences of Walras's borrowing equilibrium is the math need for fixed (conserved) quantities in Traditional Economics. This is why in such models value is a fixed quantity that is converted from one form to another: natural resources $\rightarrow$ goods $\rightarrow$ money $\rightarrow$ other goods $\rightarrow$ utility, and so on (Smith and Foley, 2002). But one should not forget the Second Law of Thermodynamics which states that *entropy* (a measure of disorder or randomness in a system) is always increasing. The Traditional model was created with the implicit assumption that the economy is a closed equilibrium system (a system with no interaction or communication with any other system, that is, no energy flowing into or out of it). Instead, the economy is not a closed equilibrium system. On the contrary, it is an open disequilibrium system, and more specifically, a complex adaptive system. Complex Adaptive Systems (CAS) are systems of interacting agents that adapt to each other and to the environment. CAS are a sub category of open systems. They need energy in order to sustain order and create complex patterns.

Obviously, it is true that economists have built models with less-than-perfect rationality, with imperfect information, with market frictions, with dynamics, and with endogenous treatments of formerly exogenous variables. Nevertheless, there is no model that relax all of these assumptions at once and, therefore, look like a real economic system. To do this, one has to abandon the idea that the economy is an equilibrium system.

2.3   What is Complexity?

There exists a growing strand of literature on complexity. This approach to science is expected to *"define the scientific agenda for the 21st century"*, according to George Cowan, founder of the Santa Fe Institute. Complexity theory is influencing several diverse fields of science. A non complete list of topics comprises physics (Anderson, 1995), cosmology (Carr, 2001), (Sylos Labini and Pietronero, 2001), chemistry (Whitesides and Ismagilov, 1999), geography (Malanson *et al.*, 2006), public transportation networks (Lu and Shi, 2007), climate research (Rind, 1999), zoology (Boyd, 2007), biology (Weng *et al.*, 1999), evolutionary biology (Parrish and Edelstein-Keshet, 1999), cell biology (Troisi *et al.*, 2005), neuroscience (Koch and Laurent, 1999), clinical medicine (Strand *et al.*, 2005), epidemiology (Pearce and Merletti, 2006), natural landform patterns (Werner, 1999), economic geography (Martin and Sunley, 2007), ecology (Grimm *et al.*, 2005), agriculture (Parker *et al.*, 2003), (Balmann, 2000), (Berger, 2001), finance (Stanley *et al.*, 2002), management (Gummesson, 2006), and economics (Arthur, 1999), (Durlauf, 2005), etc.

Definitions of *"complexity"* vary widely. In daily life parlance, something is commonly considered as complex if its behavior is difficult to be understood or if something is difficult to be dealt with. The Merriam-Webster Online Dictionary[5] defines as "complex" something *"composed of two or more parts"* or something *"hard to separate, analyze, or solve"*. Looking at the etymology of the word, it comes from Latin *complexus*, past participle of *complecti*, which means to embrace, comprise (a multitude of objects).

It derives that for a system to be complex, it has to have many parts. But simple systems also are formed out of parts. In order to have a better understanding of the differences between simple and complex systems, a more useful definition of the word "complex" could be: *"consisting of interconnected or interwoven parts"*[6]. It follows that the difference between simple and complex systems lays on these two features of a complex system *"interconnected"* and *"interwoven"*. A complex system is a blend of its parts, the behaviour of a complex system is a blend of the behaviours of its parts. But to understand the behaviour of a complex system it is not enough to understand the behaviour of its parts. It is essential the understanding of how the parts act together to form the behaviour of the whole. We cannot describe the whole without describing each part, but we must describe each part in relation to all the other parts. It is this characteristic of complex system that makes them difficult to understand, which brings us to the first definition of complex systems.

According to the Calresco Glossary[7] complexity is *"the interaction of many parts, giving rise to difficulties in linear or reductionist analysis due to the non-linearity of the inherent circular causation and feedback effects."*. Therefore, in order to have complexity we need to observe a system with many components interconnected such that would be objectively difficult to isolate them. A feature of complex system is the non-linearity and the presence of positive feedback which

---

[5] www.m-w.com

[6] complex (n.d.) The American Heritage® Dictionary of the English Language, 4th Edition. Retrieved August 30, 2007, from Dictionary.com website: http://dictionary.reference.com/browse/complex

[7] http://www.calresco.org/glossary.htm

leads to unpredictable results.

Another definition of complex system, which focuses on a their particular characteristic, is the following one from Whitesides and Ismagilov (1999): "[...] *a complex system is one whose evolution is very sensitive to initial conditions or to small perturbations, one in which the number of independent interacting components is large, or one in which there are multiple pathways by which the system can evolve. Analytical descriptions of such systems typically require non-linear differential equations.*"

Since the focus in the present work is on social systems, i.e systems whose members interact among them regularly forming a unified whole, an intuitive definition of a *"complex system"* could be the one given by Pavard and Dugdale (2000): *"A complex system is a system for which it is difficult, if not impossible to reduce the number of parameters or characterizing variables without losing its essential global functional properties."* In complex systems the interaction of the components gives rise to regularities that can not be individuated among the members themselves. This characteristic is called *emergence* (see Figure 2.1). For example a whirlpool emerges as the molecules of water interact. One can not have a whirlpool with a single water molecule. The whirlpool is a collective or emergent property of the system.

Many natural, artificial and abstract objects or networks are complex systems. Examples of complex systems include ant-hills, human economies, climate, nervous systems, cells and living things, including human beings, as well as modern energy or telecommunication infrastructures.

2.3.1 Complex versus Complicated

Complex does not necessarily mean complicated, though the two concepts are used as synonyms in common language. While complex suggests the unavoidable result of a necessary combining and does not imply a fault or failure, complicated applies to what offers great difficulty in understanding, solving, or explaining. In fact, digging up the meaning in the etymology, it comes out that *"complicated"* (cum + plicatus) has as a root the Latin *"plic"* which means "to fold", "to hide". Instead, *"complex"* (cum + plexus) contains the Latin root *"plex"* that means "to weave". Many complex systems are also complicated systems. But a complicated system is not necessary complex.

2.4 The Agent-Based Modelling Approach to Social Sciences

Agent-based object models offer a new theoretical way in order to explore the complex adaptive social systems. Like any theoretical tool these models have their advantages and disadvantages. Obviously, no single theoretical tool is suitable for all needs. Nevertheless, their comparative advantages prove to be particularly well suited in allowing us to better understand the types of problems that arise in the study of complex adaptive social systems (see Table 2.1 taken from Miller and Page (2007) to whom we refer in the following analysis).

TABLE 2.1 – *Agent-based modelling versus mathematical traditional tools*

Traditional Tools	*Agent − Based Objects*
Precise	*Flexible*
Little process	*Process oriented*
Timeless	*Timely*
Optimizing	*Adaptive*
Static	*Dynamic*
$1, 2,$ *or* ∞ *agents*	$1, 2, \ldots, N$ *agents*
Vacuous	*Spacey/networked*
Homogeneous	*Heterogeneous*

Let us begin discussing the above features. One of the most important features of any theoretical tool is its trade-off between flexibility and precision. A model is considered to be flexible when it manages to capture a wide class of behaviours. On the other hand, a model

31

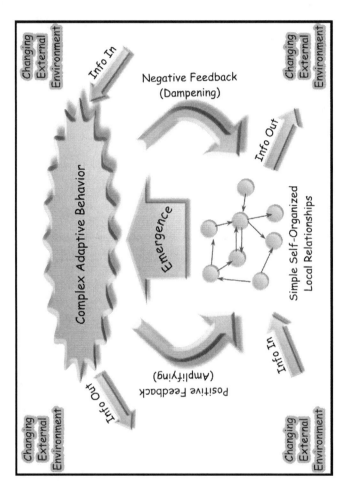

Figure 2.1 – Complex Adaptive Systems.

is precise when its elements are exactly defined. One way to achieve the highest level of flexibility is to use long verbal descriptions of the phenomena of interest. This way is a well established tradition in economics beginning from the seminal work of Adam Smith nearly two centuries and a half ago. Nevertheless, this approach suffers from ambiguity and the lack of precision. Precision, instead, is a characteristic of mathematical tools. Mathematical techniques allow the scientist to define a set of phenomena precisely and then solve the resulting system by means of a standard set of solution methods. It is clear that often the cost of such grade of precision is the lack of flexibility in the phenomena that the scientist would want to explore. Employing this set of solution means having the components of the model pure enough so that can be easily manipulated. The risk in this approach stands in the fact that by simplifying the parts of the model too much the system that is being studied may turn to be of little interest or application.

Computational models represent a good trade-off between flexibility and precision. On the one hand, computational models are remarkably flexible in their ability to capture a variety of behaviours. On the other hand, computational models require a high degree of precision. The economic system may be well encoded by a general computer language. In economics, almost all the phenomena could be studied by the mean of computer programmes which will contain all the information about the assumptions of the model in a compact and logical form. All the aspects of agents interaction must be well specified: when to act, with whom to interact and the set of the possible actions. Moreover, a specification of the information which could be accessed by each agent is needed. Furthermore, the scientist should specify how the agents may use the available information, how to cope with simultaneous decision taking processes etc..

The above mentioned is another feature of the agent-based modelling, that is, it is very process oriented. If we consider, for example, the model described in the next chapter (3), we will see that such a model requires us to carefully define each aspect of agents interaction. We define how and when agents (in our case households, firms or banks) act and with whom they interact. Moreover, we define the set of possible actions and decisions to be taken. We specify what information each agents has access to, how it can use that information etc.

Such issues are often ignored in mathematical models. In fact, a good way to get an idea on the lack of process precision employed in traditional modelling is to take a standard model and implement it computationally. Programming such models is often an enlightening experience in terms of the amount of process we ignore when we use traditional tools (Miller and Page, 2007).

Traditional models require the agents to be homogeneous. This homogeneity is a modelling necessity (or technique) rather than a real feature of the world. Moreover, traditional models are simplified in their calculations by strong assumptions on the symmetry of social systems even when asymmetry is a distinctive feature. Computational models that use agent-based objects can easily incorporate heterogeneous agents and make room for asymmetries.

Furthermore, such models are easily scaled, that is, once we describe the behaviour of a single agent, we can try to explore the behaviour of systems by simply adding more agents to the system. Being able to manipulate easily the scaling of our models may promote the discovery of key scaling laws for complex adaptive systems (Miller and Page, 2007).

Another feature of agent-based models is that they are repeatable and recoverable. Indeed, they provide some unique opportunities as an experimental medium (Miller and Page, 2007). Unlike real world experiments, computational models could be run and rerun each time we find an anomaly in the model. The initial state of the system can be recovered and the system can be observed from new perspectives in order to reveal the cause of the anomaly. This ability to rerun and reprove a system facilitates the rapid development and refinement of theoretical ideas (Miller and Page, 2007). Furthermore, we can also repeat several times the experiment on the same model without changing the initial state or run the model with slight alterations in the parameters.

Computational methods are proving to be more advantageous than the traditional ones in terms of costs. Due to decreasing costs of software, hardware and, in general, of computational power, building and running computational experiments has become cost effective. It is true that the fixed costs of developing the initial computational model could be high, but the marginal costs of running or modifying it are rather low. Once the model is developed it is easy to run it as much as it is sufficient.

2.5 Some antecedent ABM models

As we have already mentioned above, the agent-based strategy is being increasingly applied to the economics. Here we present some of the (most recent) antecedent models which have shaped the path we are walking on.

2.5.1 Evolutionary Models

An important strand of economic literature that has made use of the agent-based modelling and simulation is the Neo-Schumpeterian economics. The use of ABM techniques by Neo-Schumpeterians dates back to Nelson and Winter's work, published in 1982[8].

Nelson and Winter introduced a two-step approach to the empirical validation of simulation models. The first step involved the identification of emergent properties, or the stylized facts, that the model is expected to replicate (typically macro-level phenomena), while the second step assesses whether the model can provide further insight into economic processes. Their approach to simulation modelling has become the norm amongst neo-Schumpeterian simulation modellers, while some key elements of the Nelson and Winter model became a de-facto standard for them (Windrum, 2004). The key elements comprise the heterogeneity of the agents within a population, a selec-

---

[8]a review of the most important Neo-Schumpeterian models is found in Windrum (2004) from whom we have borrowed the description of the N&W model

tion mechanism, and a novelty generation mechanism that maintains variety in the population over time. In Nelson and Winter model different productivity of the production techniques is the key factor of firms heterogeneity. Each firm operates with one technique in every point in time and produces a homogeneous consumption good. This assumption precludes product innovation. Consumer demand is also assumed to be homogeneous in the model and the market price is exogenously given. Since the consumption good is homogeneous, firms' performance and the market selection are driven by the relative efficiency of the alternative technologies. Firms' selection process is such that firms using more efficient production techniques can offer lower prices for the standard good (and increase their market share), while inefficient firms with higher prices would eventually exit the market. The last element of the model is the open-ended search for new, more efficient production techniques. Such techniques, of above-average efficiency, would allow firms to be more successful (or at least to survive).

A number of authors have modified and extended the original model of Nelson and Winter. For a discussion on these model we remind the work of Windrum. Here we will discuss one of those contributions. In two similar papers (Dosi *et al.* (2005a) and Dosi *et al.* (2005b)) Dosi, Fagiolo and Roventini present a model of industry dynamics which yields *"endogenous business cycles with 'Keynesian' features"*. This models depicts an economy composed of firms and consumers/workers. There are two industries. The first one performs R&D and produce heterogeneous machine tools. The second industry invests in machines and produces a homogeneous good for consumption. In line with the empirical literature on investment patterns, the authors assume that the investment decisions by firms are lumpy and constrained by their financial structure. Another feature of the model, common to a growing body of literature, is the bounded rationality on the formation of expectations. There is also a capital market, assumed to be imperfect and with credit rationing, though it is not properly modelled. The rationing of credit derives from imposing a ceiling to the availability of credit to the firm through a (exogenous) maximum debt/sales ratio.

The model manages to replicate several 'stylized facts', spanning from aggregate fluctuations to regularities at micro level. Indeed, the authors find that the investment in the economy is more volatile, and consumption is less volatile than the 'GDP'; investment, consumption and change in inventories are pro-cyclical and coincident variables; aggregate employment is pro-cyclical while unemployment is anti-cyclical; firm size distributions are right skewed and firm growth-rate distribution is tent-shaped. The authors stress the fact that the observed statistical properties of the variables do not depend on the specification of the model about expectation formation. In their words *"it is the heterogeneity among the agents which is crucial to generate dynamic properties."*.

2.5.2 "Complex AdapTive System" Models

The Complex AdapTive System Models , better known as CATS (or C@S) model, has been extensively used in the last years. Under the lead of Mauro Gallegati of *Università Politecnica delle Marche* in Ancona and Domenico Delli Gatti of *Università Cattolica* in Milan, the CATS research group has been extremely successful in exploring new paths in economics. In what follows we take a look to some of their main achievements[9].

Gallegati, Delli Gatti, Di Guilmi and Giulioni (2003a) present a very simple agent-based model in which firms are heterogeneous in terms of size and degree of financial fragility and interact through the credit market. The model, an extension of Gallegati *et al.* (2003b) and Delli Gatti *et al.* (2003) consists of only two markets: goods and credit. In the goods market, output is supply driven. Firms can sell the entire amount of production they choose. Firms adopt a linear technology whose only input is capital. The output follows the evolution over time

---

[9]when we refer to the CATS model, we are in fact referring to a group of models, which sometimes are simple extensions to previous models. Nonetheless, each of them has its own peculiarities. In a more appropriate way, we should refer to it as the CATS Project

of the capital stock, which is determined by investment. The later one depends on the interest rate and the degree of financial fragility since firms take into account the risk of bankruptcy in their decisions. There is only one bank in this economy, whose role is to supply credit to the firms. The demand for credit is related to investment expenditure and therefore it depends on interest rate. On the other hand, the equilibrium interest rate for each firm depends on the bank's and firm's capital. In spite of the fact that the model is, in the words of the authors, "skeletal", it reveals his capability of replicating several empirical regularities which characterize the emergent behaviour of a system of non coordinated interacting agents.

Another important contribution comes from Delli Gatti *et al.* (2005a) where the authors show that the power law distribution of firms' size is at the root of the Laplace distribution of growth rates. Furthermore, they demonstrate that many features of business fluctuations, such as shifts of the distribution of firms' size over the cycle and many others, are a consequence of the right skewed distribution of firms' size.

In Delli Gatti, Gaffeo, Gallegati and Palestrini (2005b) the authors make use of a version of the CATS model to investigate some central issues of monetary policy. They offer a model of an adaptive complex economy populated by three classes of agents - firms, workers and banks - operating in three markets, in which a policy authority (central bank) tries to stabilize fluctuations in aggregate output and inflation. The authors evidence the importance of clear rules in the management of the central bank monetary strategy.

The acronym C@S is mentioned for the first time in Gaffeo *et al.* (2007) and the model is extremely simplified in its decisional rules. In the article the authors provide a critical assessment of the methodological solution endorsed by mainstream macro economists who try to reconcile individual behaviours and aggregate economic phenomena through the General Equilibrium analysis. Then they briefly discuss the alternative methodology, i.e the Agent-based constructive approach concluding with the description of the model and simulation results. The model consists of firms, workers and banks who operate in three markets (goods, labour and credit). What is striking is the fact that some very important decisions on prices and production of firms are taken with simple rules of thumb. Nevertheless, the model has a good capacity of replicating empirical evidence.

To conclude we would mention a recent application of the CATS model. In Russo *et al.* (2007) the model is not only used to check its capability of replicating stylized facts, but it is transformed into a computational laboratory in order to run an experiment on the role of fiscal policy in increasing macroeconomic performance.

This book builds on this huge amount of work and its important results and should be considered as part of the CATS Project. What we add to the is a model that takes on board as a whole most of the previous single extensions. Moreover, the model has a new sector (and a new market) that produces Investment Goods, in addition to the three canonical sectors/markets (Consumption Good, Labour and Credit) of the latest versions of the CATS model. We build also on the important work of Dosi, Fagiolo and Roventini whose insights we gratefully acknowledge. What we believe to be another novelty is the fact that in our model all the markets are explicitly modelled as local markets where transaction take place at an individual level.

2.From the Classics to CATS Models. A Short Story

3
A Model with Heterogeneous Interacting Agents

"...if a system ever does reach equilibrium,
it isn't just stable. It's dead"
John Holland[1]

3.1 Introduction

In this chapter we present a multi-sectoral CAS model. The model has been kept simple on purpose[2], in order to show that a rather simple non-linear framework can generate a rich set of stylized facts. Nevertheless, there is a high grade of complexity in the model itself[3]. The model describes an economy composed of firms, households and banks. Firms belong to two distinct industries. There is an upstream industry which performs R&D and produces machines/production tools (let us call them Investment Goods) by means of high skilled human resources (white collars - engineers). And there is a downstream industry which produces a homogeneous non storable good (call it

---

[1]quoted in Waldrop (1992, p. 147)

[2]at least, we tried to do so

[3]In fact, passing from a mono-sectoral model to one with two good producing sectors by adding up the upstream sector increased the complexity of the model.

41

Consumption Good) by means of low skilled human resources (blue collars - workers) and machines/production tools. Households offer their labour in the Labour Market and try to fully spend their income (wage or salary) in the Consumption Good.

3.2   The Model

We consider a sequential economy[4] populated by a large number of firms F, a large number of Households (which are made of workers - consumers) H and Banks (B). We distinguish two kinds of firms operating within two distinct branches of industries: a downstream industry made of firms (F^d) producing a homogeneous Consumption Good (CG) and an upstream industry whose firms (F^u) produce heterogeneous Intermediate (or Investment) Goods (IG). Obviously, the total number of firms in the economy is $F = F^d + F^u$.

All the agents undertake decisions at discrete times $t = 1, \ldots, T$ on the markets for the Investment and Consumption Goods and labour and credit services.

Each firm is run by a single manager, and all of them share the following characteristics. Firstly, they use decision rules with bounded rationality. This means that managers do not maximize any production function. Rather, firms choose prices and quantities in an adaptive way by looking at their most recent past. Secondly, managers try to finance their operating costs, at first, from internal funds. If these funds do not cover the whole costs, firms ask for loans to the Banks in the Credit Market.

Three kinds of markets are involved: a Labour Market (LM), a Goods Market (GM) and a Credit Market (CM). The Goods Market is subdivided into two markets: the Consumption Good Market (CGM) and the Investment Good Market (IGM). The model reproduces a *vertical* economy since the F^u firms produce IG and invest in R&D, while F^d firms buy technological innovations on the intermediate good market (IGM) to produce their output for the consumption

---

[4]in the sense of Hahn (1982)

good market (CGM) (Figure 3.1).

All markets are characterized by decentralized search and matching processes. Interactions and adjustments involve dynamics at the individual level. Macroscopic regularities emerge from the interactions of the agents at micro levels. Thus, due to the absence of market-clearing mechanisms, the economy is characterized by the contemporaneous presence of persistent involuntary unemployment, unsold production and excess of individual demand.

We suppose that firms in the downstream industry (F^d) produce the CG using technological innovations (IG) from the upstream industry firms (F^u) and low skilled workers. On the contrary, F^u firms produce IG using high skilled workers[5]. Moreover, we suppose that F^u operate under 'just in time' rules[6]. Firms and Workers interact in the Labour Market and the previous assumption requires this market to be split into two sub-markets: a high skilled workers' labour market (LM^{hs}) and a low skilled workers' labour market (LM^{ls}).

In the CGM there is an interaction between F^d and H as consumers. While in in the IGM there is an interaction between F^d in the role of customers and F^u as IG suppliers. As we will see further ahead, this increase in the productivity of the production machines is the direct consequence of R&D investments, which are financed with proper funds by the firms. The F^d's demand for IG is driven, firstly, by the necessity to replace the depreciated capital, and, secondly, by the ambition to expand its capital in order to satisfy the demand expectations. The F^d's IG demand is financed through both, own capital and credit. In general, the firms interact in the CM with the banks because, since wages are paid in advance, firms may face a liq-

---

[5]Aghion and Howitt (1992) present a model where skills of workers do matter for the production of IG, but do not for the production of CG

[6]in this model we consider the consumption good as perishable, that is, firms take note of the unsold production and then destroy it with no additional costs. In a work-in-progress version of the model we consider the consumption good as non perishable. In this case, F^d firms will operate under 'just in case' with inventories. Therefore, the unsold production enters in the balance sheet of the firm, increasing its net wealth.

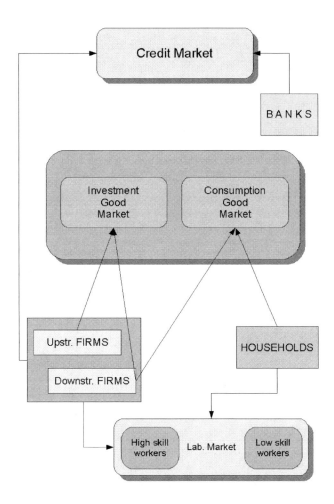

Figure 3.1 – The multi-sectoral model scheme.

uidity shortage and apply for short-term loans in the Credit Market to cover wage bill expenses. Moreover, downstream firms (F^d) try to get credit to buy new machines when they cannot manage to cover investment costs with own capital. The access to the CM for all firms will be determined by their performance on the market[7]. Besides the already mentioned vertical direction, there is also a horizontal direction into the model, that of demand and supply. This dimension is transversal to the whole model (see Table 3.1).

---

[7]a more sophisticated version of the model may take into account firms' performance in the Financial Market (which is absent in the model). This may well be an extension of the model that will need further research in the future

Market	Demand Side	Interaction	Supply Side
Labor	Downstream industry	$F^d \rightarrow LM^{ls} \leftarrow H^{ls}$	Low skilled workers
	Upstream industry	$F^u \rightarrow LM^{hs} \leftarrow H^{hs}$	High skilled workers
Goods	Consumers	$H \rightarrow CGM \leftarrow F^d$	Downstream industry
	Downstream industry	$F^d \rightarrow IGM \leftarrow F^u$	Upstream industry
Credit	Firms	$F \rightarrow CM \leftarrow B$	Banks

TABLE 3.1 – *The Multi-Sectoral Demand-Supply Scheme*

To complete the scheme, we notice that Households (H) interact with Firms (F) in the LM supplying labour to earn a wage/salary. Even though we have two kind of workers (high skilled engineers and low skilled workers), in the LM^{hs} and LM^{ls} sub-markets the matching mechanism will be very similar.

The wage is assumed to be completely spent in consumption[8]. If the consumer does not succeed in spending the whole income, he saves what remains for the following period. To keep it simple, there is no interest gain on this amount of money.

3.3 The Agents

In this section we resume the role of the Agents which are present in this simplified economy. According to their role the Agents are divided into Active Agents and Passive Agents. The former take decisions while the latter do not.

Active Agents:

- Households

  Consumption Goods Market: Role of Buyer

  Labour Market: Role of Worker

- Investment Good Producers

  Investment Goods Market: Role of Seller

  Labour Market: Role of Employer

- Consumption Good Producers

  Consumption Goods Market: Role of Seller

  Labour Market: Role of Employer

---

[8]It may be integrated with financial instruments in CM in the hand of Banks, like assets linked to the financial performance of Firms, but at the moment the model does not provide any financial market

47

- Banks

  Credit Market: Role of Credit Supplier

  Passive Agents:

- Central Bank

  Decides the highest interest rate in the credit market

- Institute of Statistics

  calculate inflation rate, unemployment, etc.

3.4 Sequence of Events

The sequence of events occurring in each time period $t = 1, \ldots, T$ runs as follows:

Event 1 *Financial Viability of Firms*

At the beginning of period t, firms check their financial viability as inherited from the past, and either they continue to operate, if their Net Wealth is positive, or they shut down due to bankruptcy, if their *NW* or *Liquidity* (in the case of Downstream firms) is lower or equal to zero. In the latter case, a string of new firms equal in number to the bankrupted ones enter the market. The process of replacement will be discussed further ahead (see 3.12).

Event 2 *Upstream - Downstream Matching*

Downstream firms perform a market research in order to find a supplier of machines/production tools . A contract will be signed between the two firms. The duration of the contract will last one period[9]. The choice of the supplier depends on the price the supplier will apply considering the average market price of machines/production tools in the district where the downstream firm operates.

---

[9]the effects of longer duration of such contracts have been investigated in the simulations of the model

Event 3 *Upstream firms' R&D activity*

Investment Good firms perform Research and Development activities. Such activities are labour saving. Firms invest in such activity part of their profits.

Event 4 *Consumption Good Sector Production Decisions*

Consumption Good sector firms take decision on production and investment. On the basis of expected demand on their goods, firms decide how much to produce and, as a consequence, how many capital and labour they need.

Event 5 *Downstream firms' Investment decisions*

Consumption Good firms decide on the investment in new machines/production tools. Normally, firms in this sector decide to expand their capital if their expected future demand is higher than their production capacity.

Event 6 *Investment Good Sector Production Decisions*

Investment-good sector takes decisions on production and investment. As already mentioned, this sector operates on the basis of a 'just in time' rule.

Event 7 *Labor Market for Engineers*

A completely decentralized labour market opens. Upstream firms set their wage bids as a function of their past wage and productivity improvements, and post their vacancies on the basis of their labour demand. Engineers, in turn, accept the job if they are unemployed. The rule is: take it or leave it. There is not bargaining on wages in the Labour Market. Nevertheless, wage can never be lower than a minimum sectoral wage decided by the trade unions (and updated periodically to take count of the inflation). A sequential matching procedure determines whether unfilled vacancies and unemployed workers remain after the labour market has closed.

49

Event 8 *Downstream Firms' Labor Demand*

Downstream firms' demand for workforce will depend on the quantity of physical capital to be run, on the expected demand for Consumption Goods and on the productivity of labour and of capital.

Event 9 *The Credit Market*

All firms calculate their financial needs and apply for loans to banks in the credit market.

Event 10 *Upstream firms' production plan revision*

Upstream firms revise their production plans considering their resources.

Event 11 *Investment Good Production and Delivery*

After being produced, the Investment Goods are delivered to the downstream firms.

Event 12 *Blue Collars' Labor Market*

Downstream firms also open positions and post them in the Labour Market. The latter shares similar characteristics with the white collars' Labour Market: there is not bargaining on the wage and there is a minimum wage which is updated periodically.

Event 13 *Downstream firms' production plan revision*

Downstream firms revise their production plans taking into account the capital and liquid funds availability.

Event 14 *Consumption Good Production*

Production of the Consumption Good takes the whole period t, regardless of the scale of output. At the beginning of each period, firms pay their wage bill in order to start production.

Event 15 *Consumption Good Market*

After the production process has been terminated, the market for Consumption Good opens. It is a posted price market. Consumers ramble around their local market for good deals. Once they have found the best deal in their local market they try to spend the whole income at the firm's offering the best deal shop. If the consumer did not manage to spend all the money at the first shop he/she will visit the second best price shop and so on.

Event 16 *Revenues, Profits, Net Worth*

Firms collect revenues, calculate profits and update their net worth.

3.5   The Consumption Good Sector

Production in this industry is carried out by means of a constant returns to scale technology, which employs labour $L_{i,t}$ and capital $K_{i,t}$ as inputs. Firms in this sector produce a homogeneous good. They choose in an adaptive way both the quantity of output to be produced and the price. As regards the price, we assume that firms operate in a posted offer market. The reader must pay attention to the fact that, despite the good being homogeneous, asymmetric information and search costs imply that the consumer can buy from a firm regardless of its price being the lowest. It follows that the law of one price does not necessarily apply (Stiglitz, 1989).

The level of production planned by the ith firm $Y_{i,t}^d$ depends on its expected demand (D^{exp}) and on the firm's productive capacity (Y^*) and is calculated as follows:

$$Y_{i,t}^d = min[D_{i,t}^{exp}, Y_{i,t}^*] \qquad [3.1]$$

Expectations on total orders to be received are taken adaptively according to the following rules.

Rule One

We will call the first one the Myopic Rule, i.e. demand expectations are revised adaptively from the firm according to the very near past effective demand:

$$D_{i,t}^{exp} = D_{i,t-1}^{ef} \qquad [3.2]$$

where $D_{i,t-1}^{ef}$ is the effective demand of goods in the previous period.

Rule Two
Managers want to produce using the whole production capacity of the firm. Therefore the desired demand will be calculated as follows:

$$D_{i,t}^{exp} = Y_{i_1,t-1}^{*} \qquad [3.3]$$

Rule Three
According to the following rule, expectations on future demand are based adaptively on the average of Sales in the past:

$$D_{i,t}^{exp} = mean(Q_{i,t-1}, Q_{i,t-2}, \ldots) \qquad [3.4]$$

Rule Four
Firms use a very adaptive rule to form their belief on future demand considering both their unsold production and their price with respect to the market price level (i.e. the CPI).

$$D_{i,t}^{exp} = \begin{cases} \overline{Y} + Y_{i_1,t-1}(1 + \xi i,t) & if \quad S_{i,t-1} = 0 \wedge p_{i,t-1} \geq CPI_{t-1} \\ \overline{Y} + Y_{i_1,t-1} & if \quad S_{i,t-1} \geq 0 \\ \overline{Y} + Y_{i_1,t-1}(1 - \xi i,t) & if \quad S_{i,t-1} > 0 \wedge p_{i,t-1} \leq CPI_{t-1} \end{cases}$$
$$[3.5]$$

where $\overline{Y}$ is the lowest quantity of output a firm would like to produce (set equal to all firms) and ξ is a uniformly distributed parameter in the $[0, 0.1]$ support.

The downstream firms' production capacity function is calculated by the means of a *Leontief* production function:

$$Y^*_{i_1,t} = min[\alpha_{i_1,t} L_{i_1,t}, \gamma_{i_1,t} K_{i_1,t}] \qquad [3.6]$$

3.5.1 The investment in new production tools

In order to calculate the production capacity of the firm, managers need to know the level of capital. In the Consumption-Good industry, firms decide to expand their stock of capital following a rule of prudence, i.e. firms will try to fill the probable gap between expected demand and previous production capacity, but in so doing, they will be limited by a fixed quantity of capital expansion.

$$\Delta K_{i_1,t} = min \begin{cases} \dfrac{D^{exp}_{i_1,t} - Y^*_{i_1,t-1}}{\gamma} \\ \text{trigger} * K_{i_1,t} \end{cases} \qquad [3.7]$$

Firms try to increase their stock of capital in order to satisfy an increasing expected demand (shall the latter be larger than the production capacity). The capital of the firm depreciates in each period at a rate δ. So in each period we have the firm's level of capital:

$$K_{i_1,t+1} = (1 - \delta)K_{i_1,t} + \Delta K_{i_1,t} \qquad [3.8]$$

Knowing the level of capital stock, Consumption-Good firms' managers determine the number of job openings:

$$L^d_{i_1,t} = a_{i_1,t} * K_{i_1,t} \qquad [3.9]$$

where a is the Capital-Labour ratio:

$$a_{i_1,t} = \frac{\gamma_{i_1,t}}{\alpha_{i_1,t}} \qquad [3.10]$$

The firm updates its Net Wealth according to nominal profits in the previous period $\Pi_{i_1,t-1}$:

$$NW_{i_1,t} = NW_{i_1,t-1} + \Pi_{i_1,t-1} \qquad [3.11]$$

3.5.2 Price Formation

Rule One:

Firms set prices considering both the unsold goods in the last period and the cost incurred in production. More precisely, let $u_{i_1,t}$ be firm's unitary cost of production. We can define the average cost for a downstream firm as follows:

$$u_{i_1,t} = \frac{I_{i_1,t} + W_{i_1,t}^{ls} + r_{i_1,t} B_{i_1,t}}{Y_{i_1,t}} \qquad [3.12]$$

where $W_{i_1,t}^{ls}$ is the Wage Bill, $r_{i_1,t}$ is the interest rate and $r_{i_1,t} B_{i_1,t}$ is the interest on debt. Firms in this sector decide the price according to the mark-up[10] rule:

$$p_{i_1,t} = (1 + \mu) u_{i_1,t} \qquad [3.13]$$

where μ is the mark-up[11] and $u_{i_1,t}$ is the average cost. Such price may be considered as the lowest price at which firms cover production costs (and perhaps make a small profit).

Rule Two:

Firms set the prices in a totally adaptive manner considering the past prices and the sales (and as a consequence the unsold production):

$$p_{i_1,t} = \begin{cases} p_{i_1,t-1}(1 + \psi_{i_1,t}) & if \quad S_{i_1,t-1} = 0 \wedge p_{i_1,t-1} \leq CPI_{t-1} \\ p_{i_1,t-1}(1 - \psi_{i_1,t}) & if \quad S_{i_1,t-1} > 0 \wedge p_{i_1,t-1} > CPI_{t-1} \end{cases}$$
$$[3.14]$$

where ψ is a random variable uniformly distributed in the interval $[0, 0.15]$ and $S_{i_1,t-1}$ is the unsold production of firm i_1 in the previous period.

---

[10] in order to reduce the overall complexity of the model we decided to adopt the same mark-up for all the firms in both sectors.

[11] $\mu \geq 0$

3.6 The Investment Good Sector

In this section we describe how the sector that produces Investment Goods operates. Firms in this sector sell their latest generation of products. This sector employs high skill labour as the unique production factor under constant returns to scale. The assumption that no physical capital is used for the production of the investment good may appear too much restrictive and simplifying. Nevertheless, it is in line with assumptions made in the new growth theory literature like in Aghion and Howitt (1992). Moreover, other agent-based models with separate investment goods sector make use of such assumptions (see for example Dosi *et al.* (2005b), Dosi *et al.* (2005a), etc.).

Upstream firms' production function will be:

$$K_{i_2,t} = \beta_{i_2,t} L_{i_2,t}^{hs} \qquad [3.15]$$

where $\beta > 0$ is the labour productivity coefficient and $L_{i_2,t}^{hs}$ is the amount of labour an upstream firm hires on the LM^{hs}. The unit cost of production is specific to the firm and depends on the Wage Bill, debt service and R&D:

$$u_{i_2,t} = \frac{RD_{i_2,t} + W_{i_2,t}^{hs} + r_{i_2,t} B_{i_2,t}}{K_{i_2,t}} \qquad [3.16]$$

where $W_{i_2,t}^{hs}$ is the Wage Bill, $r_{i_2,t}$ is the interest rate and $r_{i_2,t} B_{i_2,t}$ is the interest on debt. Firms set the price as a mark-up (z) on their unit cost of production:

$$P_{i_2,t} = (1 + z) u_{i_2,t} \qquad [3.17]$$

where $z \geq 0$ is the mark up.

Firms in the sector bear the costs of production at the beginning of the production process. As a consequence, they finance production with their stock of liquid assets (NW_{i_2}). Should the internal resources be not sufficient, firms may apply for a loan to the Banks in the Credit Market. Having determined the level of production (in the form of

55

orders from the Downstream firms), the number of job openings set by manager i at period t is given by:

$$L_{i_2,t}^d = \frac{K_{i_2,t}^{ordered}}{\beta_{i_2,t}}$$ [3.18]

At the beginning of period t, each firm is endowed with internally retained resources or Net Wealth (NW) which obeys to the following law of motion:

$$NW_{i_2,t} = NW_{i_2,t-1} + \Pi_{i_2,t-1}$$ [3.19]

The firm updates its Net Wealth according to nominal profits in the previous period $\Pi_{i_2,t-1}$.

3.7   The Consumption Good Market

Aggregate demand equals total wages paid by firms to their employees, as we assume that workers express individual demand functions with a unitary marginal propensity to consumption. Given the lack of any market-clearing mechanism and that bargains on the Consumption-Good market are fully decentralized, consumers have to search for satisfying deals. The information acquisition technology is defined in terms of the number of firms (Z) a consumer can visit without incurring any cost. In other words, search costs are equal to null when the consumer enters the market, continue to stay null if he remained confined in his local market of size Z, but they become prohibitively high as soon as the consumer tries to search outside.

Consumers enter the market sequentially, being the picking order determined randomly in every period. Each purchaser k is allowed to visit Z firms in order to detect the price posted by each of them. Prices (and the corresponding firms) are then sorted in ascending order, from the lowest to the highest. Consumer k tries to spend all his income in goods of the firm offering the lowest price in his local market. If the most convenient firm has not enough production to satisfy k's needs, the latter tries to spend his remaining income by buying from the firm with the second lowest price, and so on. If the kth consumer does not succeed in spending all his income after having visited Z firms, he saves what remains for the next period.

After the market for the consumption good has closed, the i_1th firm has received orders for $D_{i_1,t}$, but it has made sales for $Q_{i_1,t}$ at the price $p_{i_1,t}$. Accordingly, firm i_1's revenues are equal to $p_{i_1,t}Q_{i_1,t}$.

3.8   The Investment Good Market

In this section we give an overview on how the Capital Good market operates. Firms in this sector produce on demand, that is, they sell the whole number of machines produced. As a consequence, their competitiveness depends on the price they charge on the machines they put in the market.

$L_{i_2,t}^{hs}$ is the amount of labour hired on LM^{hs} by an Upstream firm. The output of the Upstream firms is an intermediate good, a kind of capital, for the Downstream firms needed to produce the Consumption Goods. Upstream firms operate 'just in time' without inventories, while the downstream firms operate considering in their decision for future production the unsold production from the past period. Coefficient $\beta_{i_2,t}$ is the high skill labour productivity. If an upstream firm do not manage to fully satisfy its orders it reduces the delivered quantities by a fraction $q = K^{produced}/K^{ordered}$

3.8.1   The Upstream - Downstream Matching Mechanism

Equation (3.6) states that a downstream firm's demand signal matches only one upstream firm supply. This is a simplification that can be done if one assumes that all the upstream firms produce the same intermediate good: in real world's economy things are more complicated since each firm needs different kind of intermediate goods as in a Leontief like model. To let the model be more realistic, we introduce a kind of selection process in terms of prices to let a downstream firm

57

to match with only one upstream firm[12]. There is a kind of supply relationship between a downstream firm and an upstream firm. The downstream firm carries out market research activities in the district where it operates. The district consist of the nearest x upstream firms, randomly chosen for the moment (in terms of distance, in the future). The downstream firms choses the Investment Good supplier that offers the best (lowest) price. Once the downstream firm has chosen its upstream supplier a contract is signed. This kind of contract remain valid for a fixed number of periods. The reason is that there exist very high costs for changing the machines supplier. The downstream firm tries to maintain the relationship with the chosen upstream firm until the opportunity cost do not turn to be very high[13].

3.9 Profits

Nominal profits in the downstream industry are defined as follows:

$$\pi_{i_1,t} = p_{i_1,t}Q_{i_1,t} - W_{i_1,t}^{ls} - I_{i_2,t} - r_{i_1,t}B_{i_1,t} - RD_{i_1,t} \qquad [3.20]$$

where Q_{i_1} is the amount of sales, $W_{i_1}^{ls}$ is the Wage Bill of the low skilled workers and I_{i_2} are the new investments in machines/production tools.

The profits of the upstream firms read like follows:

$$\pi_{i_2,t} = P_{i_2,t}K_{i_2,t} - W_{i_2,t}^{hs} - r_{i_2,t}B_{i_2,t} - RD_{i_2,t} \qquad [3.21]$$

where $P_{i_2} * K_{i_2}$ are the Revenues, $W_{i_2}^{hs}$ is the Wage Bill of the high skilled workers, B_{i_2} is the debt amount and RD_{i_2} is the R&D spending.

---

[12]in a new version of the model we will introduce the distances between firms in terms of transportation costs or other typologies of distance

[13]we are simulating several duration periods of the validity of the contract

3.10   The Labour Market

The Labour Market in our model is not a conventional one, i.e. one characterized by rational individual agents who supply and demand labour services according to the level and flexibility of the real wage rate. In this economy the relevant variable is the monetary wage. Its level is the result of firms' decisional process which takes place in an individual level at the beginning of each production period before the current prices of the consumption good have been determined.

Firms and workers form their expectations about the level of these prices, but they do not know *ex ante* the level of the real wage rate. Therefore, the level of the monetary wage is periodically reviewed. In so doing, firms take account of historical path dependence and adapt to the reality.

As has been already mentioned, there are two distinct labour markets in our model. There is one labour market for engineers and one labour market for unskilled workers. Engineers work in the upstream industry that performs R&D and produce production tools that need to be developed, while the blue collars work in the downstream firms.

Firms[14] set their labour demand on the basis of their desired level of production. Though the two sectors of the economy are distinct and different, the way they hire their employees is very similar. Each firm decides autonomously the wage level and opens vacancies according to the production needs. The unemployed people read the vacancies and apply for the position. Thus, the firm creates a queue of open positions. We assume that the H workers supply inelastically one unit of labour per period. Moreover, the contracts last one or more than one period (in simulations we have considered contract durations of more than one period).

The matching mechanism in the labour market is such that a worker k can visit sequentially at most M firms. The first one is the firm where he/she worked in the previous period if he/she was

---

[14]For recent examples of agent-based computational macroeconomic models where the labour market is analyzed along similar lines, see Fagiolo *et al.* (2004a), Delli Gatti *et al.* (2005a), Russo *et al.* (2007) etc.

employed. The other $M - 1$ are chosen at random at any period t. Worker k is hired by the firm only if the firm has still open vacancies. If worker k is not hired by firm i, he/she continues to the next firm already chosen.

The wage offered by a generic firm i in period t is calculated according to the following rule:

$$w_{i,t} = \begin{cases} max\left\{w_{i,t-1}, w_{i,t-1}(1 + inf_{i,t}) * \Delta lab.prod.\right\} & if \quad L_{i,t-1} < L_{i,t-1}^d \\ w_{i,t-1} & if \quad L_{i,t-1} = L_{i,t-1}^d \end{cases}$$

$$[3.22]$$

where $L_{i,t-1}$ is the number of workers actually employed in $t - 1$. According to equation 3.22, firm's last wage bids are revised upward if in the last period the search for labour force was not entirely successful, that is, if not all posted vacancies were filled in. Wages offered are left unchanged if the firm managed to hire all the people it needed. In any case, the wages in each period can not be lower than in the previous period[15]. Moreover, there is a minimum wage decided by law. Firms can not offer wages lower than the minimum wage.

Finally, the production plan and, consequently, the desired hiring policy, can be realized only if the firm has enough financial resources. If this is not the case, the firm's plans are revised until labour cost does not violate the financial constraint. Firms would fire the employees receiving the higher wages. Workers fired because of this process remain unemployed for the whole period t. Due to such characteristics of the model the labour market results to be very flexible.

3.11 The Credit Market

Our credit market has been built along the lines of the Monetary Circuit Theory mostly developed by Augusto Graziani (see for example Graziani (2003)). According to this theory, entrepreneurs (firms) are

---

[15] in the case of deflation wage bids would have been lower than in the previous period.

the unique economic agents who have access to bank credit. Potentially they can borrow an unlimited amount of means of payment. On the contrary, workers do not have access to bank credit. They receive money wages from firms for the supply of their labour-power. Therefore, they only have at their disposal as much monetary purchasing power as they have earned. The banking system plays an important role in this economy in that it is placed both at the starting and at the end of the monetary circuit. In each period, banks first create and then destroy the total amount of bank money.

The organization of the monetary circulation in the economy implies that, since production takes time and workers (wage-earners) have to be paid before sales are made by firms, firms may need loans before work can commence. In order to run the planned production, upstream and downstream firms may find themselves in shortage of liquidity. Since firms in this economy are financially constrained in the equity market, if the internal liquidity of firms is insufficient to pay in advance the whole Wage Bill, the costs of R&D and/or the Investment in new machines of firms then firms turn to the credit market. Banks offer loans and this creates credit money[16]. When sales occur, firms charge prices which generate a profit for each of them and also make it possible to repay the loan, with interest determined by a bargaining process between banks and firms[17]. At this point, the credit money originally created ceases to exist and the monetary circuit is complete.

Credit demand of each firm is equal to labour, investment (in the case of the Downstream firms) and R&D costs excess over its financial resources (or reserves). We have that:

---

[16]we assume that there is a risk coefficient, i.e. a threshold ratio of equity to credit, that banks try to target, either because of discretional strategies of risk management or as a consequence of prudential regulation on the part of the monetary authority. Therefore, the aggregate supply of credit from the banks turns out to be a multiple of their equity. We have called it, improperly, the multiplier

[17]even though in our model firms have no power in the bargaining process. They behave as price takers and accept the interest rate offered them by the banks

$$B_{i_s,t} = (Total \;\; Cost_{i_s,t} - A_{i_s,t}) \qquad [3.23]$$

Firms borrow at a fixed interest rate, $r_{i_s,t}$ at the beginning of the period. The payment is carried out at the end of each period in a fixed number of installments[18]. Firms that do not manage to pay back their debt go bankrupt. The lending bank suffers a bad debt equal to the difference between lent money and the part of the debt paid back.

Each firm (upstream or downstream) will contact a certain number of $\mathcal{K}^*$ banks in a random way. Each bank will ask a different rate of interest $r_{k,t}$[19]. Firms will start to borrow from the bank offering the lowest interest rate. We assume that firm i_s will ask inelastically the amount $B_{i_s,t}$.

3.11.1 Firm - Bank Interaction

The amount of credit the firm i_s will require at the beginning of period t is given by Eq. (3.23). Firms may apply to a maximum of $\mathcal{K}^*$ banks for credit in order to increase their chances of a positive outcome, but the credit demand is indivisible and each firm could obtain the credit only by one bank. Firms have no information regarding banks' dimensions.

Suppose $\varphi_{i_s,t}$ to be an indicator of the *financial health* of the single firm. A bank can ask for this information in order to decide whether to lend money, or not. Among other indicators, we may use the *Return on Sales - ROS* index which is the ratio of profits on the value of sold production (which may be $Q_{i_1,t}$, or $Q_{i_2,t}$ according to the industry a firm belongs to).

$$\varphi_{i_s,t} = \frac{\pi_{i_s,t}}{Q_{i_s,t}} \qquad [3.24]$$

---

[18]since firms may be indebted to acquire Investment Goods which normally would last for several periods, we allowed firms to repay back the loan in several installments

[19]the number of banks in the economy is $\mathcal{K}$ with $\mathcal{K}^* \leq \mathcal{K}^*$

with $s = 1, 2$. So the firm i_s gives the vector of known past informations up to time $\tau \in \mathbb{T} = \{t_0, t_1, \ldots, t - 1, t\}$ to banks from which it hopes to borrow money

$$\Phi_{i_s} = (\varphi_{i_s,\tau})_{\tau \in \mathbb{T}} \qquad [3.25]$$

Assume the *volatility* to measure uncertainty and, as such, providing a measure of risk up to time t

$$v_{i_s,t} = \mathbb{V}\left(\Phi_{i_s}\right) \qquad [3.26]$$

Banks can compute the *expected volatility* of the *ROS* index known up to time t about a firm i_s since they have the vector $v_{i_s,t} = (v_{i_s,\tau})_{\tau \in \mathbb{T}}$

$$\hat{v}_{i_s,t+1} = \mathbb{E}_t(\mathbf{v}_{i_s,t}) \qquad [3.27]$$

No banks in the CM possess all the information vectors about all the firms. This means that not all banks have the single firm matrix $V_t = \{\mathbf{v}_{i_s,t} : i_s \in \mathcal{A}_s\}$. Nevertheless every bank knows the *average volatility* on the market up to time t:

$$\bar{v}_t = |\mathcal{A}_s|^{-1} \sum_{i_s \in \mathcal{A}_s} v_{i_s,t} \qquad [3.28]$$

and the *average expected volatility*

$$\hat{\bar{v}}_t = |\mathcal{A}_s|^{-1} \sum_{i_s \in \mathcal{A}_s} \hat{v}_{i_s,t+1} \qquad [3.29]$$

is a shared information among banks, but only a small number $\mathcal{K}^* < \mathcal{K}$ have access to micro data of the kind V_t, where $\mathcal{K}$ is the number of all banks.

If $\hat{v}_{i_s,t+1} > \bar{v}_t$ a bank refuses to lend money to the firm i_s, otherwise the matching bank-firm happens in this way. A firm asks for money (demand) to $\mathcal{K}^*$ banks, each of them answers (potential supply) with a price (the required rate of interest) and the firm chooses the bank with the lowest price. The banks' price setting rule, based on uncertainty ratios, is the following:

$$r^{\otimes}_{i_s,k,t} = \rho_k \left(\frac{\hat{v}_{i_s,t+1}}{\bar{v}_t} \right) \qquad [3.30]$$

The price is enclosed within the unit circle as long as the banks' specific parameter $\rho_k \in (0,1)$. This parameter can be seen as a control variable from the point of view of the bank: it can be seen as a banks' dimension measure or a risk aversion index. The price reflects the idea that the higher the uncertainty ratio the higher the price will be.

3.12   The process of firm's replacement

At the end of every period, firms with negative Net Wealth (or left without liquid monetary resources) go bankrupt and are replaced by new firms. The entry process in the literature is modeled either as a purely stochastic process (see for example Winter *et al.* (2003)), or as an endogenous process, in which the number of entrants depend on the current profit (Hopenhayn, 1992). The process of replacement of bankrupted firms follows a simple rule. For both industries (the one that produces machines and the one that produces a good for consumption) we compute the average values of productive capital, wage bids, etc. of the surviving firms (i.e with positive Net Wealth $\overline{NW}_{i_2} > 0$, in the case of the Upstream sector, and positive liquid resources $\overline{CASH}_{i_1} > 0$ in the case of the Downstream sector). We give to the entrants the average values of surviving firms. Hence, the number of firms in both sectors remain constant across time.

3.13   The Process of Research and Development

The economy is characterized by a permanent process of technical change. As already mentioned, both Capital-Good firms and Consumption-Good firms perform Research and Development (R&D) activities. In each period, besides producing and selling their machines and the consumption good, Upstream and Downstream firms try to develop new and better ways of producing their goods.

First of all let us define the R&D functions in both branches of the industry. We consider the fact that the value of R&D investments is given by a fixed fraction σ_1 and σ_2 of nominal profits which are defined from eq. (3.20) and eq. (3.21) respectively. So the R&D investments' value are given by:

$$RD_{i_1,t} = \sigma_1 \pi_{i_1,t-1}$$
$$RD_{i_2,t} = \sigma_2 \pi_{i_2,t-1} \qquad [3.31]$$

If profits in period $t-1$ have been null (or negative) then the firms do not perform R&D activity.

Productivity coefficients for the firms can be supposed to follow some AR(1) processes, far from the unit root case. We start from the productivity coefficient in the upstream industry. Its law of motion is the following:

$$\beta_{i_2,t+1} = \beta_{i_2,t} + \lambda_t \qquad [3.32]$$

where λ is a random number drown from an exponential distribution with mean $RD_{i_2,t}/P_{i_2,t}K_{i_2,t}$.

Productivity coefficients for the downstream firms evolve according to the following law:

$$\alpha_{i_1,t+1} = \alpha_{i_1,t} + \zeta_t \qquad [3.33]$$

$$\gamma_{i_1,t+1} = \gamma i_1, t + \xi_t \qquad [3.34]$$

where ζ_t and ξ_t are drown from a random process, exponentially distributed with mean $1/2 RD_{i_1,t}/p_{i_1,t}Y_{i_1,t}$[20].

---

[20]Russo *et al.* (2007) uses the same random process. An alternative could have been to use a first-order autoregressive process with estimated parameters like the following:

$$\alpha_{i_1,t+1} = \phi_0 + \phi_1 \alpha_{i_1,t} + \zeta_t$$

The normalization factor ($P_{i_2,t}K_{i_2,t}$ or $p_{i_1,t}Y_{i_1,t}$) allows the effect of R&D investments on firm's productivity to be independent of the scale of production.

$$\gamma_{i_1,t+1} = \psi_0 + \psi_1\gamma_{i_1}, t + \xi_t$$

with ψ_0, ψ_1, ϕ_0 and ϕ_1 being estimated parameters and ζ_t and ξ_t drown from a standard normal random process with zero mean and constant variance. A first tentative is made in Bianchi *et al.* (2007a)

4
The Model vs. Stylized Facts

"The whole is more than the sum of its parts."
Aristotle

4.1 Introduction

In this chapter we will present and discuss the results of the simulations of the model presented in Chapter 4 and those of a simplified version. As we will see, the model is able to generate a viable economy and manages to replicate some stylized facts. In Sections 4.2 and 4.3 we discuss the results of the simplified model, while the complete model will be discussed in Section 4.4, where we show some additional evidence on the ability of the model to replicate empirical facts. Lastly, in Section 4.5 we perform some robustness checks and discuss how the model responds to departures from the initial values of some of the variables.

4.2 Baseline Model Simulation Results

In this section we present in detail the results of the simulations of the model. We begin with simulation results of a baseline model without R&D activities from the firms. The following results derive from a single execution of the model of 3000 periods. In most of the figures which will be presented below the first 100 periods are not shown. In other words, we have cut off the transient dynamics of the model. Simulations of the baseline model have been run for the following choice of parameters and initial values for the variables (see Table 4.1).

F^u	100
F^d	300
J^{hs}	150
J^{ls}	750
$Banks$	2
A^{firm}	20
A^{bank}	50
w_{hs}^{min}	2
w_{ls}^{min}	1
$job\ applications\ M$	3
$shops\ visited\ Z$	3
$district\ dimension$	1
p	1
P	1
α	1
γ	1
β	0.5
$money$	1
$trigger$	0.01
δ	0.1
$max.\ int.\ rate$	0.15
$official\ discount\ rate$	0.02
$mark-up$	0.01

TABLE 4.1 – *Initial values*

The reader must bear in mind that we are merely interested in assessing the qualitative features of the model. Therefore, the model has not been calibrated at all.

4.2.1 Emerging Dynamics

As one may expect, without improvements in productivity, the economy rapidly stabilizes and then continues to fluctuate along a steady state path. The Figure 4.1 displays the annualized Aggregate Output (we may call it GDP) and the Output's growth rate of the Downstream sector[1]. The GDP moves in the long-run along a stable corridor.

The average growth rate of the economy[2] in the entire time span, $T = 1-3000$, is equal to 0.015%, but it is very near to zero if we do not consider the initial growth[3]. Since the growth rate of the population in our model is equal to zero (we keep the number of the households constant) this result is in line with the Traditional economic growth models.

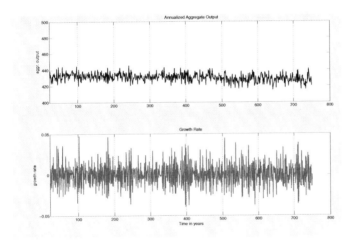

Figure 4.1 – Annualized Aggregate Output (GDP) and its growth rate

---

[1]If we consider one simulation period to correspond to three months then four simulation periods would correspond to the year. Therefore, Figure 4.1 depicts an annual time series.

[2]we have used the following formula: $av.gr.rate = \frac{logY_T - logY_1}{T}$

[3]the average growth rate of the aggregate output is 0.049% in the first 1000 periods time span, it is -0.0019% in the second one thousand periods and -0.0022% in the last span

Figure 4.2 depicts the total production of the two sectors of the economy (upstream and downstream) in a logarithmic scale. Moreover, the bottom panel of the figure depicts both the effective production and the production capacity of the downstream sector.

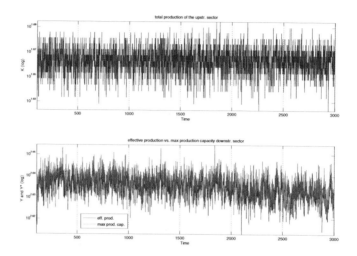

Figure 4.2 – Aggregate Output of Downstream (Y) and Upstream K firms (in logs)

The effective production follows the path of the maximum production capacity (the correlation coefficient is $\omega = 0.9844$). Firms manage to adapt their demand expectations in order to be very near to the full capacity production level. The figure 4.3 shows in the top panel the same graph of the Figure 4.2, while the bottom panel shows a zoomed in part of the effective production and of the full production capacity series [4].

The growth rate of the production of the Upstream sector is characterized by a higher volatility with respect to the production of the Downstream sector. This is due to the fact that the Upstream sector produces on demand. Therefore it is characterized by periods of low

---

[4]in this simulation we have calculated the Expected Demand of the firms according to Rule Four

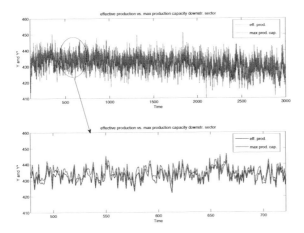

Figure 4.3 – Effective Aggregate Output vs. Production Capacity

activity followed by periods of high production activity. The growth rates of the output appear to follow a Gaussian walk. This assures a stable path for the output.

Prices of both, the Consumption Good and the Investment one, double in the time span of the simulation (Figure 4.4, top two panels). Consumption Good price inflation and wage inflation are characterized by stationary fluctuations in time. Wage inflation is more volatile than the price inflation. In fact, the corridor of fluctuations is twice wider for the later with respect to the former. These variables are both slightly pro-cyclical (the correlation coefficients with the output growth are $\omega = 0.0961$ and $\omega = 0.1030$ respectively).

We refer now to the bankruptcy of firms and the exit and entry process in the economy. We recall here the fact that in our model a firm in the Upstream sector goes bankrupt if its Net Wealth becomes negative. As far as the Downstream sector is concerned, things are slightly different, since here part of the Net Wealth of a firms is in the form of Investment Goods (production tools). Therefore, a firm in this sector would go bankrupt if it lost the whole liquid part of Net Wealth. There are no failures among Upstream firms and banks

71

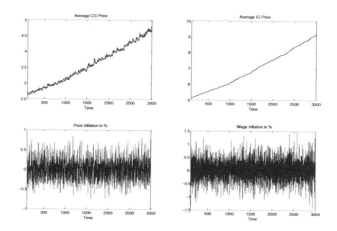

Figure 4.4 – Average Price of IG and CG and Inflation

(see Figure 4.5, top and bottom panels). The lack of failures among Upstream firms may be well explained by the fact that since firms in this sector operate on demand, they manage to plan the whole production process in advance. Moreover, upstream firms manage to sell the whole output. Local market failures cause the firms in the Downstream sector to go bankrupt. Firms in this sector face the risk of not being able to wholly (or even partially) sell their output. Therefore, some of the firms fail and exit the market. Nevertheless, the magnitude of bankruptcies is very low, in the order of 0.5 - 0.6% of the firms with some peaks that reach the level of 1% (which means 3 firms in absolute terms, see Figure 4.5, middle panel). Therefore, the risk of bad loans for the banks is very low and this explains the fact of no defaults among banks.

Figure 4.6 reports the time series of the average effective and lowest price of the Consumption Good[5]. Even though firms decides the price through a very simple and routinized procedure that considers only past unsold stocks and the Consumer Price Index, interestingly

---

[5]what we call here the lowest price (in order to cover costs) is in fact a price equal to the average costs plus a mark-up.

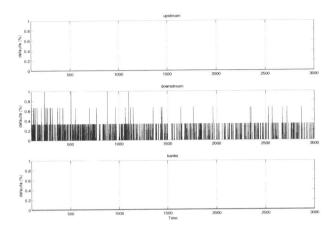

Figure 4.5 – Bankruptcy rates of firms and banks

enough, they manage to decide (on average) a price that is higher than the price that would allow them to cover production costs.

Other variables' time series characterized by stationary fluctuations are the real wages and the unemployment rates. Panels in Figure 4.7 report the real wage of the high skilled workers (top panel) and low skilled ones (bottom panel). Wages are highly correlated with the Consumption Good price. In fact, coefficients of correlation between the nominal average wages and Consumption Good price are $\omega = 0.9852$ for the LS workers and $\omega = 0.9855$ for the HS workers

The rates of unemployment for the low and high skilled workers are reported in Figure 4.8. As we have already mentioned, no calibration have been made to the model. Therefore, the apparently "non realistic for a normal economy" unemployment rates (on average 19% and 38% respectively) depend mostly on the initial conditions of the baseline model.

Figure 4.9 displays the evolution of the average real wage (left ax) and the real total profits (right ax) of the downstream firms (top panel) and upstream firms (bottom panel). It indicates that the income distribution shares remain basically constant over the whole

73

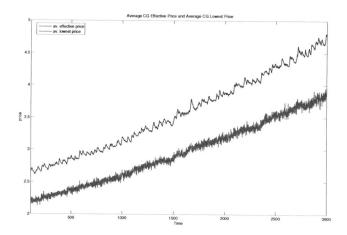

Figure 4.6 – Effective Price vs. Lowest Price of CG

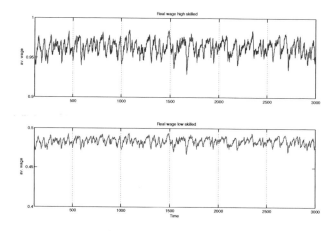

Figure 4.7 – Real Wages

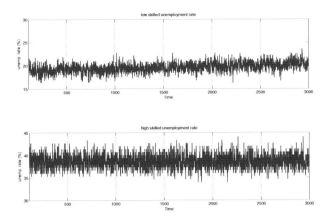

Figure 4.8 – Unemployment rates

simulation.

4.3 Macro-Micro Stylized Facts and Model's Replication

In this section we give an overview of some of the main stylized facts of the economy, i.e the Phillips Curve, The Wage Curve, The Beveridge Curve and the Okun Curve. These macroeconomic relations have been object of study for decades. Fagiolo *et al.* (2004b) discuss some of the main empirical contributions on these relations confronting them with possible results that could be obtained from evolutionary agent-based models. The authors consider the contributions from traditional model as unsatisfactory. In fact, *"notwithstanding the existence of some competing, although not entirely persuasive, interpretations of each of the three aggregate regularities* taken in isolation, *the economic literature witnesses a dramatic lack of theories attempting* jointly to explain *Beveridge, Okun and Wage curves"* (Fagiolo *et al.* (2004b), p. 10). Moreover, evidence from real data has been often

75

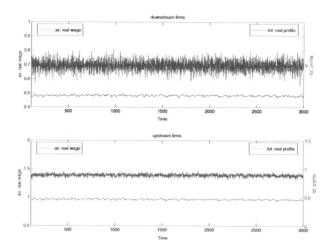

Figure 4.9 – Wage vs. Profits

controversial. In fact, the relations between the wage inflation, or the vacancy rate, and the rate of unemployment show characteristic patterns called *loops*, that is, a cyclic behaviour of the relations between the variables rather than a series of points fitted by a straight line. As we shall see further ahead, even a simplified and decentralized labour market in a single model allows the emergence of the above mentioned macroeconomic regularities.

4.3.1   The Phillips Curve

In 1958 A. W. Phillips published a study on the level of the wages in the United Kingdom in the period 1861-1957 (Phillips, 1958). The main result of that study was what we now refer to as the Phillips Curve. It is an inverse relation between the rate of unemployment and the rate of growth of monetary wages in an economy. Stated simply, the higher the unemployment in an economy, the lower will be the rate of change in monetary wages paid to labour in that economy. In other words, there exist a trade-off between wage inflation and unemployment. In the course of time the meaning of the expression "Phillips Curve" has widened. Now the terminology is used to indicate both the original curve and a relationship between the unemployment rate and the prices growth rate i.e the inflation rate.

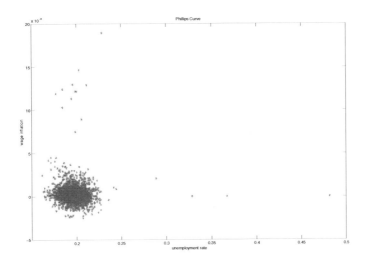

Figure 4.10 – Phillips Curve (baseline model, wage inflation)

At the height of the Phillips curve's popularity as a guide to (Keynesian) policy, Edmund Phelps and Milton Friedman independently challenged its theoretical underpinnings. They argued that well-informed, rational employers and workers would pay attention only to real wages. Thus, an expectation - augmented Phillips Curve should be found in the short run, while the long run should be characterized by a vertical Phillips Curve, in correspondence to the NAIRU or "natural rate of unemployment". Therefore, there should not be trade-off between inflation and the unemployment rate in the long run.

Many studies have investigated the existence of an expectation - augmented form, also vis-à-vis the existence of a Wage Curve, which, as we will explain in the next section, relates the unemployment rate to the absolute level of the real wages. The general conclusion is that the Wage Curve is more reliable than the Phillips Curve as a labour market regularity.

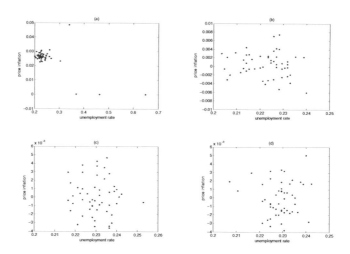

Figure 4.11 – Phillips Curve (baseline model, price inflation, periods 1 - 50 (a), 200 - 250 (b), 400 - 450 (c), 600 - 650 (d))

We begin by showing a scatter-plot of the relationship between the wage inflation and the rate of unemployment that comprises the whole simulation period (Figure 4.10). Then we consider the price inflation. In both cases, the curve depicts a negative relation between the two variables. We go now to see what happens in shorter periods of simulation. In the next two Figures (4.11 and 4.12) we present the Phillips Curves generated by our model in four different moments of simulation for each figure (periods of 50 iterations), considering the price and the wage inflation respectively. The Figure 4.13 depicts the cyclical behaviour of the relation wage inflation - unemployment rate i.e. the Phillips loops.

4.3.2 The Wage Curve

The Wage Curve describes a negative relationship between the average wage $\bar{w}$ and the unemployment rate u (Blanchflower and Oswald,

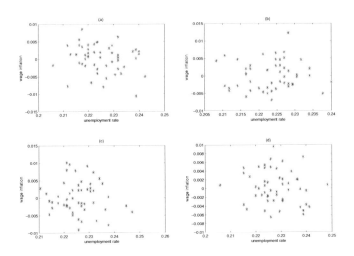

Figure 4.12 – Phillips Curve (baseline model, wage inflation, periods 250 -
300 (a), 350 - 400 (b), 450 - 500 (c), 550 - 600 (d))

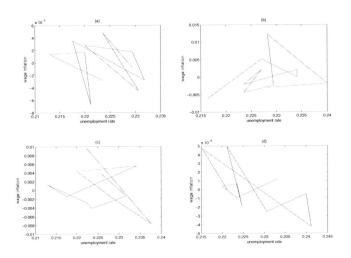

Figure 4.13 – Phillips Loops (baseline model, wage inflation, periods 290 -
300 (a), 390 - 400 (b), 490 - 500 (c), 590 - 600 (d))

1994; Card, 1995)[6]. The Wage curve, well grounded in the empirical evidence, is generally posited as one of the building blocks of imperfect labour markets. Its plausibility rests, for instance, on efficiency wages or union bargaining considerations.

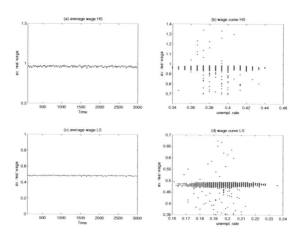

Figure 4.14 – Wage Curves

Our baseline model is not able to fully capture this fact in the very long term. Figure 4.14 depicts the average real wages of the downstream and the upstream sector (panels a and c) and the relationship between the average real wage and the unemployment rate for both sectors (panels b and d). Since the scatter plots for the wage curves do not appear to be very informative on eventual trends we check the correlation coefficients. In the case of the upstream sector the correlation is negative (ω = -0.0411), but it turns to be slightly positive in the case of the downstream sector (ω = 0.0318). Things change if we check the correlation coefficients in the downstream sector in a mid-term and in a short-term scenario. If we check the correlation between the

---

[6]in Blanchflower's and Oswald's words *"a worker who is employed in an area of high unemployment earns less than an identical individual who works in a region with low joblessness"*

wage level and the unemployment rate in the simulation period 2900-3000 it turns to be negative (ω = -0.1842) and the result improves if we take into consideration a very short simulation period, 2960-3000, which turn an ω = -0.3048. The inability of the baseline model to "produce" wage curves with negative slopes could be due to the fact that the real wages do not grow in time. Moreover, the labour markets are not subdivided into "areas" characterized by different rates of unemployment. Therefore, all the workers have "theoretically" the same chances to face (short or long) unemployment spells.

4.3.3   The Beveridge Curve

The Beveridge Curve (named after William Beveridge , 1879-1963) postulates a negative relationship between the unemployment rate and the vacancy rate. It shifts inward and outward during the transition periods. An outward shift implies then a given level of vacancies would be associated with higher and higher levels of unemployment, which would signal decreasing efficiency in the labour market, for instance due to structural adjustments of the economy.

The Beveridge Curve is an equilibrium relation theoretically derived from the assumptions on the matching function (being the analogue of an isoquant for a production function) (Pissarides, 2000). Its empirical evidence, however, is rather weak.

Figure 4.15 plots the Beveridge Curve (panel (a)) and the so called Beveridge Loops (panels (b) - (d)) with respect to different moments of the simulation.

4.3.4   The Okun Curve

The Okun Curve describes a negative, more than proportional, relationship between the changes in the unemployment rate $\dot{u}$ and the growth rate of GDP g (Prachowny, 1993; Attfield and Silverstone, 1997). The Okun Curve is mainly an empirical regularity and it is not clearly grounded in economic theory. Figure 4.16 depicts such an empirical regularity resulted from the simulation. It shows that

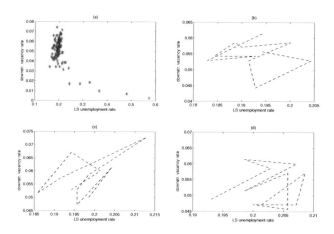

Figure 4.15 – Beveridge Curve (Downstream Sector)

our model is capable of replicating this stylized facts. The correlation coefficient is $\omega = -0.7583$ for the Downstream sector and $\omega = -0.9970$ for the Upstream sector.

4.3.5 Firms' Size Distribution

The distribution of firms' size is not normal, but it is described by a Power Law. Normally it shifts to the right during the cycle as showed by Gaffeo *et al.* (2003). There are several studies that confirm this regularity, like for example Axtell (2001), or Gaffeo *et al.* (2003) etc.. The distribution of profits also follows a Power Law as found for example in Fujiwara *et al.* (2004b), Fujiwara *et al.* (2004a), or Delli Gatti *et al.* (2003). The rates of growth of aggregate production and firms' output follow similar Laplace distributions (Stanley *et al.*, 1996).

The following figures (Figures 4.17 - 4.25) show some distributions of the growth rates and of firms' size (considering different measures of the size of the firm), while Figure 4.26 refers to the Households

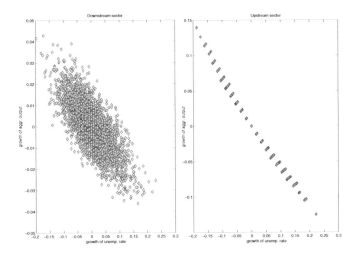

Figure 4.16 – Okun Curves

wealth distribution[7].

Figures 4.17 and 4.18 depict the distribution of the growth rates of the aggregate output for the two sectors. We performed the Kolmogorov - Smirnov, Anderson - Darling and Chi-Squared statistical tests to check for the Normal distribution of the growth rate of the Downstream Aggregate Output (i.e. the GDP). None of them rejected the null hypothesis that the data follow the specified distribution. Nevertheless, the best fit of the data is the Beta distribution[8]. Moreover, the K-S test do not reject the null hypothesis of Beta, Gen. Extreme Value, Lognormal and Weibull distributions. As for the Aggregate production growth rates of the Upstream sector, the best fit is the Normal distribution, the second best is the Logistic and the third-best the Beta Distribution. Nevertheless, all the tests reject the null hypothesis of normality. The next two figures show the downstream firms' size distribution according to two variables. The first

---

[7]the analysis of the distributions has been conducted using Matlab and EasyFit softwares

[8]the ranking of the distribution from the one that best fits the data to the worst fit has been done according to the K-S statistic

83

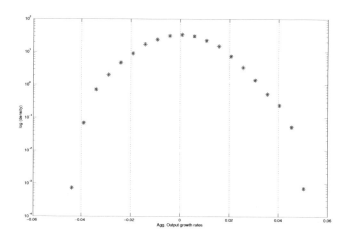

Figure 4.17 – Distribution of Downstream sector's Aggregate Output growth rate

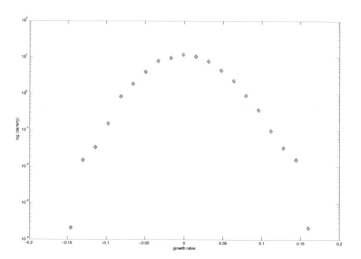

Figure 4.18 – Distribution of Upstream sector's Aggregate Output growth rate

one (Fig. 4.19) considers the total sales, while the second one (Fig. 4.20) considers the physical capital available to Downstream Firms at the end of the simulation (T = 3000). The simulated data depart from the normal distribution, showing skewed tails.

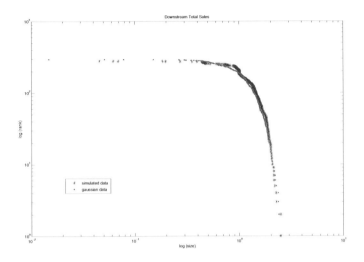

Figure 4.19 – Firms' size distribution (Downstream firms Total Sales) in period T = 3000

Figure 4.21 plots the distributions of Net Wealth for the Upstream and the Downstream sectors respectively. The distribution that best fit the data of the Downstream sector is the Gumbel Max. Then, in order, follow the Lognormal (3P), the Gen. Extreme Value, Gamma, Weibull, Gen. Pareto and so on. The Normal distribution is only the 14th best fit. In fact, the K-S test rejects the hypothesis of normally distributed data. The K-S test do not reject the null hypothesis of normality for the Upstream sector Net Wealth distribution. Nevertheless, the best fit distribution is the Gen. Pareto, followed by Gen. Extreme Value and the Weibull. The Normal distribution ranks 7th. If we plot together the data from the two sectors, their distribution turns to be Lognormal (3P), having the Gamma (3P) and Beta as the second and third best respectively and the Normal falls back at the 14th place.

85

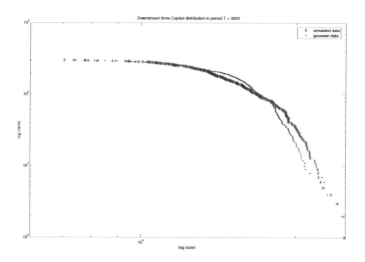

Figure 4.20 – Firms' size distribution (Investment Good available to Downstream firms) in period T = 3000

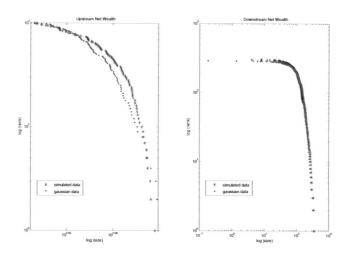

Figure 4.21 – Firms Net Wealth Distribution (Period T = 3000)

We turn now to discuss the simulation results on the profits of firms. Figure 4.22 plots the distribution of the growth rate of Profits on Net Wealth ratio of the Downstream sector. We first consider the last period of simulation and plot the data together with a normal distribution curve (red dots). A visual inspection clearly shows that the simulated data have a fatter tale than the Gaussian distribution. The distribution that best fits the data is the Laplace. In fact, the K-S test rejects the null hypothesis of normality. The same analysis performed for the Upstream sector, gives as a result the Lognormal, refuting the hypothesis of normality.

We then go further in the analysis of the data and plot the distribution of the growth rate of the Profits on Net Wealth ratio taken in three different periods of the simulation (T = 2800, T = 2990 and T = 3000). We show the results in Figure 4.23. It emerges a shift of the curve during the different phases of the cycle, a behaviour similar to that observed empirically.

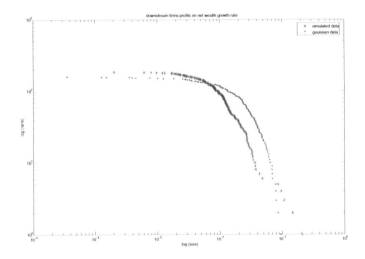

Figure 4.22 – Downstream firms Profits on Net Wealth ratio growth rate in period T = 3000 (Gaussian data in red dots, simulated data in blue pluses)

Another variable that we consider as a proxy of the size of the firms is the production. We repeat the procedure that we carried

87

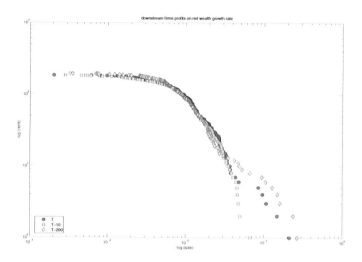

Figure 4.23 – Downstream firms Profits on Net Wealth ratio growth rate in periods T = 2800 (diamonds), T = 2990 (squares) and T = 3000 (circles)

out when we considered the profits, i.e. we first check our simulated data's distribution against the normal distribution (which has the same mean and variance as the simulated data) and then we check how the distribution shifts over time. The results attained previously are confirmed. The series exhibits a skewed distribution (Figure 4.24). Moreover, we again find that the series distribution shifts in time (Figure 4.25), but the movements are not as strong as in the case of the Profits on Net Wealth ratio.

We have checked for other proxies of firms' size. We found that the downstream firms' wage bills are distributed as a Weibull (refuting the null hypothesis of normality), while the wage bills of the upstream sector are best fitted by a Gen. Extreme Value distribution (again refuting the null hypothesis of normality). The workforce is distributed as Weibull and as Gen. Extreme Value in the downstream and the upstream sectors respectively. Even in this case the K-S test rejected the Normal hypothesis.

At the end, we take a look to the distribution of the wealth of the households. As we have already described in the previous chapter,

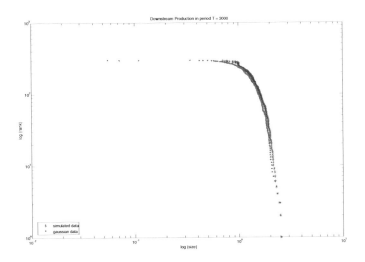

Figure 4.24 – Firms size distribution in period T = 3000 (Downstr. production)

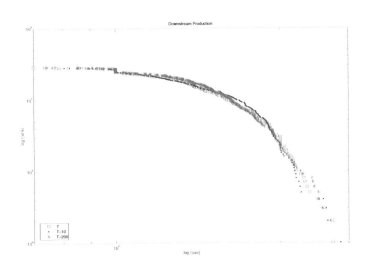

Figure 4.25 – Firms size distribution (Downstr. production) in periods T = 2800 (pluses), T = 2990 (dots) and T = 3000 (squares)

89

households begin their life with the wealth equally distributed. As time passes, households sell their labour to firms. They earn money which they try to wholly spend in consumption (we assume a savings propensity equal to zero). If they do not manage to spend the whole income, they save the money for the next period. Figure 4.26 shows the wealth of the households at the last period of simulation. Even in this case, simulated data strongly depart form the normal distribution indicating a situation where there are a few households "richer" than what they would have normally been.

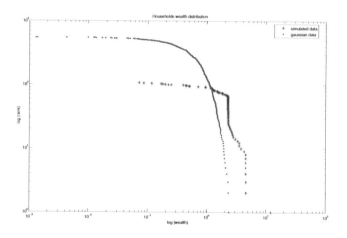

Figure 4.26 – Households Wealth Distribution (Period T = 3000)

4.4 Complete Model Simulation Results

In this section we will present some additional results derived from a simulation of the complete model described in Chapter 4. R&D and therefore, labour saving improvements of technology are the engine of growth of the economy. In fact, as soon as we allow firms to carry on research activity, the economy moves from the steady state path to an upward (growing) path of the Aggregate Output. Moreover, firms manage to adapt their expectations on future demand and, in so doing, they are able to operate near the full capacity production level (4.27).

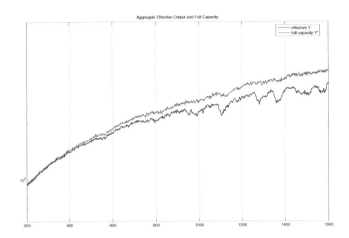

Figure 4.27 – Effective Aggregate Output versus Full Capacity level of Aggregate Production

The level of bankruptcies among Downstream firms is still low. It remains under the 2% level during the whole simulation. There are not bankrupted firms in the Upstream sector or among the banks. As we have already underlined, the fact that there are not defaults among the upstream firms could be a result of the fact that firms in this sector produce on demand and that the prices are fixed according to a mark-up rule. As for the downstream sector, firms face higher uncertainty on their future sales and expectations are built on very basic rules of thumb. Nevertheless, firms manage to fix prices in line with the level that allows them to cover average costs of production (Figure 4.28). Since there is a very low level of bankruptcy among firms (we may say at a physiological level), there are not high levels of bad debts among firms, i.e. the banking sector does not have a high exposure to bad loans and therefore there are not any bankruptcies.

The rate of unemployment of the low skilled workers is stable if

91

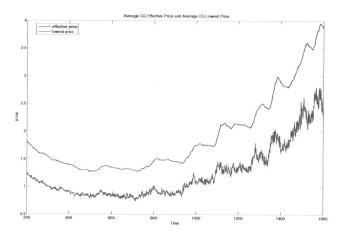

Figure 4.28 – Effective price vs. lowest price

we consider long periods of time. It is around 6% in period 200, it falls down and remains stable for a relatively long period, at the 2,5% level, and it begins to increase, as a consequence of the labour saving technology, to end up below the 10% level in period 1600. The unemployment rate of the high skilled workers is more stable in the very long period of time, but it is more volatile in the shorter ones.

The model confirms its capability to replicate some empirical regularities at a macro level. In particular it generates a positive relationship between the real wages and the productivity of labour (Figure 4.29 and Figure 4.30), the Phillips Curve (Figure 4.31), the Beveridge Curve (Figure 4.32) and the Okun Curve (Figure 4.33), whose properties have been discussed at length in Section 4.3. Moreover, the growth rate of the GDP is distributed according to a Beta distribution, though the K-S test did not reject the hypothesis of normally distributed data.

We turn to discuss some empirical regularities at firms' level. Firstly, we plot the Net Wealth of the firms in the last period of the simulation (T = 1600). As we can see from the loglog plot (Figure 4.34), the distribution of firms according to their size is right skewed,

92

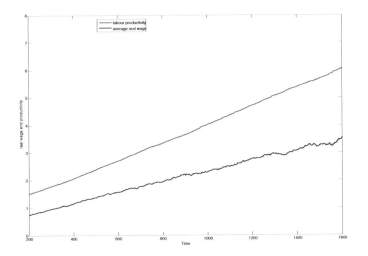

Figure 4.29 – Real Wage and Productivity

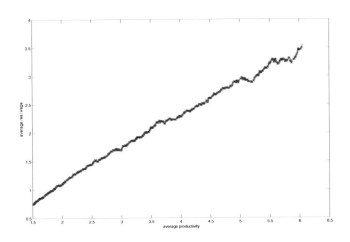

Figure 4.30 – Real Wage and Productivity

93

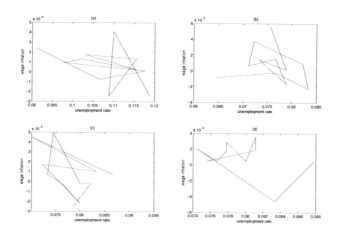

Figure 4.31 – Phillips Loops

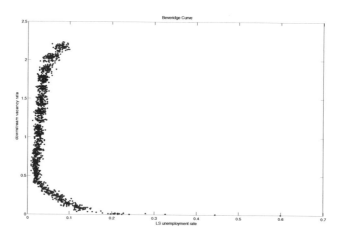

Figure 4.32 – Beveridge Curve

94

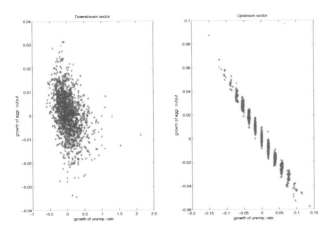

Figure 4.33 – Okun Curve

showing a fat tail which is on the right of the Gaussian distribution, a fact that has been empirically proved form several studies we have cited above. We found that the data are best fitted by a Gen. Pareto distribution[9] rejecting the hypothesis of Normality. We show the time evolution of firms' net wealth in Figure 4.35.

We found similar evidence when we considered the distribution of firms taking as a proxy of the firms' size the quantity of Capital (Investment Good) available to them in the last simulation period (Figure 4.36).

In Figure 4.37 we show the shifts to the right of the distribution of firms' size during the cycle (using the firms' production as a proxy of the firms' size). This emergent behaviour is similar to evidence from real data as has been confirmed by several studies (see for example Gaffeo *et al.* (2003)).

We controlled the distribution of several variables of interest at firms level, such as the Loan Requests, Downstream firms workforce and R&D spending in both sectors. We found that in all the cases

---

[9]with Gen. Extreme Value and Beta distributions as 2nd and 3rd best choices.

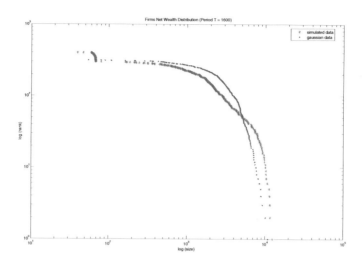

Figure 4.34 – Firms' Size distribution according to the Net Wealth in the last period (T = 1600)

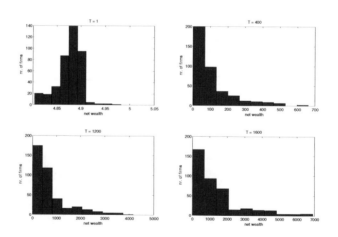

Figure 4.35 – Evolution of firms' net wealth in time

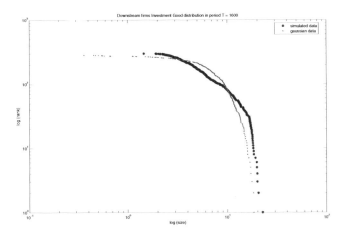

Figure 4.36 – Downstream Firms' Size distribution according to the Investment Good in the last simulation period (T=1600)

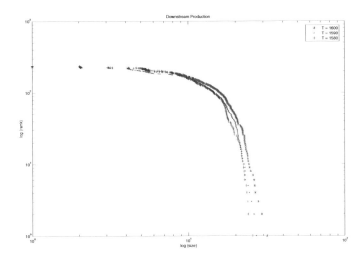

Figure 4.37 – Downstream Firms' size distribution shifts (firms' production)

the distribution that best fitted the data was the Gen. Pareto. An exception is the Upstream R&D spending which is fitted by a Weibull. Furthermore, the Upstream R&D spending was the only case in which the hypothesis of normality was not rejected by the K-S test[10].

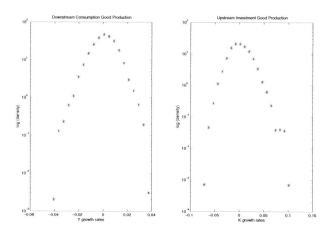

Figure 4.38 – Consumption and Investment Goods output growth rate distribution

As a last evidence on the properties of the model we show the distribution of the Households' wealth at the end of the simulation period (Figures 4.39 and 4.40). We find that even in this simplified economy, a pattern similar to the well known distribution of the income in real life, emerges from the interaction of the agents at a local level.

4.5 A further step...

The robustness of the results discussed at length in the previous sections has been checked recurring to Monte Carlo techniques. As a first step, we run 30 independent simulations for different values of

---

[10]but this hypothesis was rejected by the Anderson-Darling test

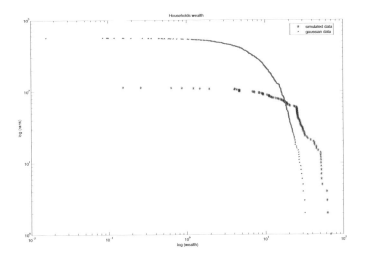

Figure 4.39 – Households wealth distribution at the last period (T = 1600)

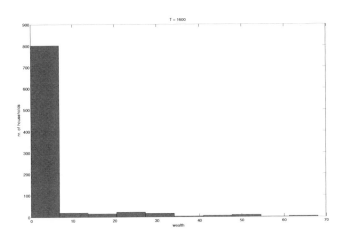

Figure 4.40 – Households' wealth at the end of the simulation

the initial state of the pseudo-random numbers generator. We then study the mean and the standard deviation of the variables of interest. Results reported in Table 4.6 confirm that our findings are indeed quite robust.

As a second step, we check the behaviour of the model to changes in one of the parameters. We run several simulation of 500 periods each. Initially we consider the searching costs in the matching process between firms in the upstream and downstream sectors (we have called it "district dimension"). We begin by allowing downstream firms to match with the first upstream it finds (the highest search costs). Then we relax this assumption allowing the downstream firms to match with the upstream firm that offers the lowest price out of a maximum of three upstream firms. A first interesting result is the effect on unemployment. Lower search costs benefit mostly the low skilled workers. Their unemployment rate falls down from 26% to 20% on average. Firms in the Downstream sector find better prices which allows them to buy more Investment Good which allows them to increase their production capacity and consequently the unemployment falls. On the contrary, the unemployment rate of high skilled resources increases from 41% to 55%. Since there is a higher selection among the Upstream firms, only the firms with higher productivity will be chosen and therefore less labour force will be required. Another consequence of lower searching costs is lower average vacancy rates in both sectors. The aggregate output of the CG at the end of the simulation increases as the searching costs decrease (passing from 1 to 3 firms), while the opposite happens for the aggregate IG output.

Moreover, we examine the effects of longer labour contract duration on the key macroeconomic variables. We run 16 simulations (8 for each sector) increasing every time the duration of contracts by one (from one to eight periods). Results are reported in Tables 4.2 and 4.3. As the duration of contracts in the Downstream sector augments, the inflation and the unemployment rate of the high skilled workers remains stable, while there is a sharp decrease in the unemployment rate of the low skilled resources. Furthermore, the growth rate of the GDP increases on average and the same effect can be found on the

100

TABLE 4.2 – *Simulated time average of key macroeconomic variables for different durations of labour contracts (downstream sector)*

$review_{dnstr.}$	1	2	3	4	5	6	7	8
$inflation$	0,002	0,002	0,002	0,002	0,002	0,002	0,002	0,002
$unemp_{LS}$	0,2049	0,1265	0,1653	0,1129	0,0977	0,0914	0,0672	0,0698
$unemp_{HS}$	0,5493	0,5449	0,5403	0,5418	0,5405	0,5398	0,5401	0,5405
Y_T	617	718	717	759	778	799	809	797
y gr. rate	0,0007	0,0008	0,0008	0,0009	0,0009	0,0009	0,0010	0,0009
k gr. rate	0,0039	0,0039	0,0039	0,0039	0,0039	0,0039	0,0039	0,0039

level of the GDP in the last period.

As far as the inflation is concerned, similar results are found when we keep the review of the contracts of the downstream sector fixed at one and increase the duration of the contracts in the Upstream Sector. In this case, there is a general drop in the unemployment rate in the economy as a whole, while y and k are more stable than in the previous case. As expected, there is a drop in the vacancy rate of the Upstream sector, while the average vacancy rate rate of the Downstream sector slightly increase. A final important result is presented by the fact that the fluctuations of the aggregate output decrease in number and magnitude. An intervention of the policy-maker in the labour legislation turns to have stabilization effects on the business cycles.

TABLE 4.3 – *Simulated time average of key macroeconomic variables for different durations of labour contracts (upstream sector)*

$review_{upstr.}$	1	2	3	4	5	6	7	8
$inflation$	0,003	0,003	0,003	0,003	0,003	0,003	0,003	0,004
$unemp_{LS}$	0,23	0,21	0,19	0,20	0,19	0,20	0,22	0,19
$unemp_{HS}$	0,38	0,36	0,36	0,35	0,35	0,35	0,35	0,34
Y_T	575	618	631	526	574	643	591	537
$v.ncy$ r. $_{up.}$	0,009	0,007	0,005	0,004	0,003	0,003	0,002	0,002
$v.ncy$ r. $_{dn.}$	0,392	0,408	0,412	0,428	0,417	0,417	0,421	0,422
y gr. rate	0,0007	0,0007	0,0007	0,0006	0,0007	0,0008	0,0007	0,0006
k gr. rate	0,0042	0,0042	0,0042	0,0042	0,0043	0,0043	0,0043	0,0043

We continue our discussion of results considering the trigger rule of capital expansion. As we have explained in Chapter 4 downstream firms decide to expand their capital according to a very simple rule: each period firms can't expand their capital beyond a certain limit which we fix at 1% of the available capital. We then keep doubling the limit on every run of the model to end up at 32% in the 6th run. The idea behind this experiment is to see how the prudence of a firm on investing its money helps the overall performance of the system. At the level of 1% firms are extremely prudent i.e. they do not raise the level of capital more than 1% of the in loco capital. At a level 32% firms do not show any prudence at all. We report some of the most interesting results in Table 4.4.

TABLE 4.4 – *Simulated time average of key macroeconomic variables for different trigger rules*

trigger	0,01	0,02	0,04	0,08	0,16	0,32
$unemp_{LS}$	0,13	0,10	0,09	0,24	0,33	0,42
$unemp_{HS}$	0,37	0,37	0,36	0,19	0,66	0,70
Y_T	1317	1484	1487	1045	914	233
K_T	127	131	129	163	52	29
y gr. rate	0,0014	0,0015	0,0015	0,0012	0,0010	-0,0001
k gr. rate	0,0042	0,0042	0,0042	0,0044	0,0034	0,0029

Passing from a highly restrictive rule of capital expansion to more and more permissive rules has two fold effects on the variables under study. As we move from a 1% limit to a 4% one, there is a general beneficial effect to the economy. The average unemployment rate falls down in both sectors, the aggregate output at the end of the simulation is higher and there is an increase of the average growth rate of the aggregate output of both sectors. As we keep increasing the limit of the trigger rule, all the effects are cancelled and at the last simulation (at a 32 % limit) the overall effect is not positive: we have a negative average growth rate of the aggregate output of the downstream sector and the unemployment rates are three and two times higher than those in the first simulation for the low skilled and the high skilled resources respectively (Table 4.4).

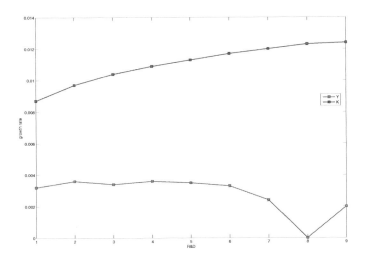

Figure 4.41 – Simulation evidence on the relationship between R&D and the aggregate output growth rate

We turn now to analyse the role of the R&D in shaping macroeconomic performance[11]. Our focus is on the relationship between the propensity of firms (in this case we consider the Upstream ones) to invest in R&D, the growth rate of the economy and the average values of some important macroeconomic variables such as the unemployment rate, the vacancy rate, the inflation rate and the number of bankruptcies. To this end we perform 9 simulations of the model with increasing levels of the R&D parameter σ_2. We start with σ_2 being a random variable uniformly distributed in the space $[0,0;0,1]$ to $[0,8;0,9]$ with 0,1 steps.

Simulations show a monotically increasing relationship between investment in R&D and the growth rate of the aggregate output of the Upstream sector. Moreover, the marginal returns of R&D activity are decreasing[12]. It seems, however, that R&D efforts in the Upstream

[11]a similar analysis has been carried out in Russo *et al.* (2007).

[12]Russo *et al.* (2007) have similar results.

sector have no impact on the aggregate output of the CG producing sector, at least, unless it reaches the level of 70% of the profits invested (Figure 4.41). Higher fractions of the Upstream profits invested in R&D correspond to higher costs of the IG, and as a consequence to lower profits for the Downstream sector and, therefore to lower Net Wealth accumulation, higher prices of the CG (Figure 4.42, panel (b)), higher financial fragility and finally to an increasing number of bankruptcies in this sector (Figure 4.42, panel (d)).

Other interesting results emerge from the simulations, such as a monotonic relationship between Upstream R&D and the Downstream sector vacancy rate; a non existent effect on the unemployment rate of the high skilled human resources; and a negative effect on the low skilled workers (Figure 4.42, panel (a) and (c)).

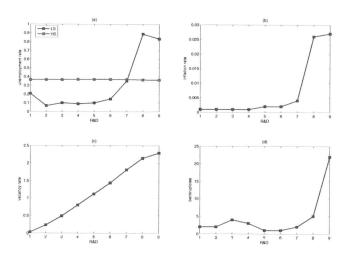

Figure 4.42 – Simulation evidence on the relationship between R&D and key macroeconomic variables: (a) unemployment rate; (b) inflation rate; (c) vacancy rate; (d) number of bankruptcies

At the end, we investigate how the searching costs in the local labour and the goods markets affect the results of the model. To accomplish this task we run 49 simulations for different combinations of the number of job applications and the number of visited shops and calculate time averages of some important variables across each simulation. We report the results in Table 4.5.

TABLE 4.5: Simulated time average of some variables for different combinations of searching costs

number of job applic.						number of visited shops	
	1	2	3	4	7	10	20
Average growth rate of Aggregate Output Y							
1	0,0011	0,0011	0,0011	0,0011	0,0011	0,0012	0,0012
2	0,0007	0,0008	0,0008	0,0008	0,0008	0,0007	0,0009
3	0,0008	0,0003	0,0007	0,0007	0,0002	0,0006	0,0007
4	0,0005	0,0003	0,0004	0,0007	0,0006	0,0005	0,0008
7	0,0005	0,0004	-0,0002	0,0001	0,0003	0,0005	0,0005
10	-0,0002	0,0003	0,0007	0,0003	0,0000	0,0005	0,0003
20	0,0003	0,0005	0,0005	0,0000	-0,0001	-0,0001	-0,0001
Average growth rate of Aggregate Output K							
1	0,0042	0,0042	0,0042	0,0042	0,0042	0,0042	0,0042
2	0,0041	0,0041	0,0042	0,0042	0,0042	0,0042	0,0042
3	0,0042	0,0041	0,0042	0,0042	0,0042	0,0042	0,0042
4	0,0042	0,0042	0,0042	0,0042	0,0042	0,0042	0,0043
7	0,0042	0,0042	0,0042	0,0042	0,0042	0,0042	0,0043
10	0,0042	0,0043	0,0042	0,0042	0,0042	0,0043	0,0042
20	0,0042	0,0043	0,0042	0,0042	0,0042	0,0042	0,0042
Average bankruptcies in the Downstream sector							
1	7	2	4	2	2	2	2
2	8	4	2	1	2	2	2
3	55	4	2	2	3	3	3
4	10	4	2	2	2	2	2
7	7	2	2	2	2	2	2
10	7	2	2	2	2	2	2
20	3	2	2	2	2	2	2
Average inflation rate							
1	0,002	0,002	0,002	0,002	0,002	0,002	0,002
2	0,003	0,003	0,002	0,003	0,003	0,003	0,003
3	0,002	0,004	0,003	0,003	0,004	0,003	0,003
4	0,004	0,004	0,004	0,003	0,004	0,005	0,003
7	0,004	0,004	0,005	0,006	0,005	0,004	0,005
10	0,005	0,004	0,004	0,004	0,005	0,005	0,005

continued on next page

Table 4.5 — *continued from previous page*

number of job applic.						number of visited shops	
	1	2	3	4	7	10	20
20	0,005	0,004	0,006	0,005	0,007	0,006	0,007

Average unemployment rate of low skilled workers

	1	2	3	4	7	10	20
1	0,077	0,055	0,067	0,049	0,066	0,054	0,060
2	0,229	0,206	0,178	0,184	0,185	0,229	0,177
3	0,176	0,316	0,227	0,208	0,386	0,225	0,234
4	0,328	0,249	0,182	0,190	0,225	0,214	0,202
7	0,287	0,262	0,294	0,222	0,241	0,213	0,237
10	0,283	0,265	0,187	0,191	0,337	0,233	0,217
20	0,250	0,220	0,221	0,286	0,305	0,278	0,188

Average unemployment rate of high skilled workers

	1	2	3	4	7	10	20
1	0,374	0,373	0,374	0,374	0,374	0,372	0,375
2	0,382	0,384	0,382	0,383	0,384	0,381	0,382
3	0,390	0,377	0,378	0,378	0,373	0,375	0,375
4	0,372	0,374	0,375	0,375	0,372	0,374	0,372
7	0,371	0,367	0,369	0,371	0,366	0,367	0,367
10	0,365	0,367	0,365	0,367	0,362	0,365	0,362
20	0,364	0,364	0,367	0,362	0,363	0,363	0,365

Average vacancy rate in the Downstream sector

	1	2	3	4	7	10	20
1	0,440	0,443	0,442	0,436	0,448	0,452	0,441
2	0,412	0,413	0,416	0,413	0,410	0,416	0,416
3	0,375	0,392	0,392	0,395	0,410	0,406	0,410
4	0,381	0,381	0,390	0,393	0,401	0,394	0,403
7	0,374	0,393	0,388	0,385	0,406	0,404	0,403
10	0,390	0,392	0,410	0,393	0,420	0,407	0,416
20	0,404	0,406	0,392	0,413	0,413	0,414	0,410

Average vacancy rate in the Upstream sector

	1	2	3	4	7	10	20
1	0,02159	0,02104	0,02151	0,02124	0,02091	0,01996	0,02216
2	0,01760	0,01799	0,01817	0,01745	0,01844	0,01677	0,01836
3	0,00961	0,00971	0,00947	0,00987	0,00945	0,00973	0,00965
4	0,00491	0,00459	0,00504	0,00505	0,00457	0,00497	0,00484
7	0,00067	0,00061	0,00073	0,00073	0,00061	0,00064	0,00087
10	0,00004	0,00012	0,00013	0,00003	0,00007	0,00012	0,00007
20	0,00000	0,00000	0,00000	0,00000	0,00000	0,00000	0,00000

Level of Aggregate Output in the last period

	1	2	3	4	7	10	20
1	894	885	890	903	917	923	931

continued on next page

Table 4.5 — *continued from previous page*

number of job applic.						number of visited shops	
	1	2	3	4	7	10	20
2	624	676	672	683	676	634	726
3	679	386	575	593	334	520	627
4	456	394	425	628	527	468	644
7	473	405	226	306	368	498	499
10	218	389	610	376	259	480	403
20	366	458	474	270	255	254	237

Low skilled minimum wage in the last period

1	1,410	1,340	1,374	1,356	1,469	1,395	1,409
2	1,438	1,429	1,412	1,448	1,486	1,490	1,480
3	2,175	1,603	1,481	1,536	1,685	1,543	1,672
4	1,633	1,648	1,693	1,685	1,605	1,826	1,542
7	1,702	1,739	1,949	2,099	1,805	1,867	1,945
10	1,668	1,805	1,723	1,882	1,879	2,086	1,865
20	1,812	1,798	2,307	2,034	2,663	2,355	2,311

High skilled minimum wage in the last period

1	2,820	2,679	2,747	2,712	2,938	2,790	2,817
2	2,876	2,858	2,825	2,896	2,971	2,980	2,960
3	4,350	3,206	2,961	3,072	3,371	3,086	3,345
4	3,266	3,297	3,385	3,370	3,209	3,652	3,083
7	3,405	3,479	3,898	4,198	3,609	3,733	3,889
10	3,336	3,611	3,445	3,764	3,758	4,172	3,731
20	3,625	3,595	4,615	4,068	5,325	4,710	4,623

Time Average of the average CG price

1	2,765	2,325	2,401	2,342	2,468	2,306	2,317
2	3,545	2,967	2,819	2,890	3,007	3,020	2,842
3	1,630	3,648	3,113	3,058	4,267	3,233	3,450
4	4,363	3,519	3,389	3,417	3,614	3,724	3,155
7	4,633	4,140	4,412	4,304	3,868	4,152	4,385
10	4,405	4,475	3,918	4,538	5,088	5,129	4,091
20	5,349	4,583	6,143	5,360	7,600	6,748	5,006

We begin the analysis of the results considering the growth rate of the Downstream sector Aggregate Output (i.e the GDP). On the one hand, it seems that lower search costs in the Consumption Good market have a rather limited impact on the aggregate growth rate. On

107

the other end, lower search costs in the labour market show a strong negative impact on the growth performance of the economy (panel 1 of Table 4.5).

As far as the Investment Good aggregate output is concerned, lower search cost in both of the markets have no appreciable consequences on its growth rate (panel 2 of Table 4.5).

High search costs in the Goods market markets have a relatively higher impact on the time average number of bankruptcies of downstream firms with respect to labour market search costs (panel 3 of Table 4.5).

In turn, different combinations of search cost levels in both markets determine large shifts of the Phillips curve: as search costs on both markets are lowered, inflation and the unemployment rate (in the downstream sector) increase (panels 4 and 5 of Table 4.5). As for the average unemployment rate of high skilled workers, it remains in the interval 36%-39% during the 49 simulations. This result means that the unemployment in the Upstream sector is due to the fact that this sector operates under the "just in time" rule (panel 6 of Table 4.5). Lower search costs are accompanied by very large fluctuations of the GDP and, as a consequence, by higher average rates of unemployment. Moreover, lower search costs mean higher competition in the goods and labour market which are echoed in higher CG prices and higher minimum wages (last three panels).

4.6   Appendix 1

The Table 4.6 summarizes the Mean and Standard Deviation (std) of variables of interest resulted from a Monte Carlo experiment. We run the model 30 times (simulations of 300 periods) changing each time the state of generator of random numbers.

TABLE 4.6: Monte Carlo estimation with different states of the pseudo random numbers generator

state	Y_T	y	π_{price}	π_{wage}	$def.$	$vac.$	LSu	HSu	k
0	427	0,0015	0,0034	0,0014	0,4733	0,0532	0,1955	0,3894	0,0007
std.	20	0,0139	0,0109	0,0096	1,0486	0,0106	0,0331	0,0390	0,0371
1	429	0,0014	0,0035	0,0014	0,6500	0,0531	0,1938	0,3886	0,0008
std.	21	0,0120	0,0109	0,0096	1,7676	0,0104	0,0343	0,0393	0,0405
2	430	0,0015	0,0036	0,0015	0,4933	0,0536	0,1887	0,3889	0,0006
std.	20	0,0121	0,0110	0,0099	1,0927	0,0108	0,0341	0,0390	0,0378
3	426	0,0015	0,0034	0,0014	0,4067	0,0531	0,1999	0,3882	0,0005
std.	20	0,0136	0,0109	0,0094	0,8268	0,0106	0,0337	0,0385	0,0334
4	430	0,0014	0,0035	0,0014	0,4700	0,0539	0,1911	0,3875	0,0008
std.	21	0,0124	0,0108	0,0096	0,9445	0,0103	0,0343	0,0389	0,0359
5	425	0,0015	0,0035	0,0015	0,5600	0,0544	0,1992	0,3879	0,0008
std.	20	0,0126	0,0109	0,0096	1,2669	0,0106	0,0322	0,0393	0,0379
6	421	0,0013	0,0035	0,0014	0,4767	0,0529	0,2102	0,3879	0,0005
std.	18	0,0127	0,0109	0,0098	0,8114	0,0106	0,0306	0,0388	0,0363
7	430	0,0015	0,0033	0,0013	0,4000	0,0541	0,1873	0,3880	0,0008
std.	21	0,0124	0,0109	0,0092	0,8300	0,0106	0,0353	0,0390	0,0359
8	431	0,0014	0,0034	0,0014	0,4467	0,0532	0,1891	0,3889	0,0006
std.	21	0,0132	0,0108	0,0094	0,8423	0,0110	0,0345	0,0388	0,0368
9	426	0,0014	0,0034	0,0014	0,6467	0,0534	0,1984	0,3891	0,0008
std.	21	0,0127	0,0109	0,0095	1,4975	0,0111	0,0349	0,0388	0,0363
10	428	0,0014	0,0034	0,0014	0,5333	0,0533	0,1940	0,3881	0,0005
std.	21	0,0131	0,0110	0,0097	1,2862	0,0107	0,0343	0,0390	0,0358

continued on next page

109

Table 4.6 — *continued from previous page*

state	Y_T	y	π_{price}	π_{wage}	def.	vac.	LSu	HSu	k
11	431	0,0014	0,0033	0,0013	0,5133	0,0542	0,1880	0,3873	0,0005
std.	21	0,0123	0,0108	0,0097	1,0803	0,0111	0,0345	0,0385	0,0357
12	431	0,0015	0,0035	0,0014	0,4300	0,0536	0,1886	0,3880	0,0006
std.	21	0,0132	0,0109	0,0093	0,9317	0,0112	0,0346	0,0385	0,0361
13	430	0,0014	0,0035	0,0015	0,4633	0,0542	0,1911	0,3877	0,0005
std.	21	0,0131	0,0109	0,0095	0,9264	0,0106	0,0340	0,0385	0,0338
14	431	0,0014	0,0035	0,0015	0,5033	0,0535	0,1885	0,3873	0,0005
std.	21	0,0115	0,0109	0,0097	1,1018	0,0104	0,0334	0,0384	0,0341
15	430	0,0014	0,0034	0,0014	0,3433	0,0548	0,1925	0,3861	0,0007
std.	21	0,0133	0,0107	0,0096	0,6055	0,0109	0,0346	0,0388	0,0352
16	417	0,0014	0,0035	0,0014	0,5267	0,0529	0,2150	0,3892	0,0007
std.	18	0,0137	0,0109	0,0094	0,9122	0,0106	0,0313	0,0385	0,0353
17	419	0,0014	0,0034	0,0013	0,6000	0,0526	0,2133	0,3882	0,0007
std.	19	0,0124	0,0108	0,0095	1,1992	0,0102	0,0315	0,0387	0,0352
18	427	0,0014	0,0034	0,0015	0,5467	0,0543	0,1985	0,3881	0,0007
std.	21	0,0134	0,0110	0,0095	1,2273	0,0111	0,0343	0,0384	0,0336
19	429	0,0014	0,0035	0,0014	0,4800	0,0540	0,1912	0,3875	0,0005
std.	21	0,0125	0,0108	0,0097	1,0864	0,0107	0,0343	0,0386	0,0352
20	431	0,0015	0,0033	0,0014	0,4267	0,0532	0,1892	0,3880	0,0009
std.	21	0,0128	0,0108	0,0093	0,8166	0,0104	0,0343	0,0391	0,0376
21	432	0,0015	0,0034	0,0014	0,4233	0,0534	0,1884	0,3872	0,0007
std.	21	0,0124	0,0108	0,0095	0,7343	0,0104	0,0343	0,0388	0,0355
22	424	0,0014	0,0034	0,0014	0,6367	0,0546	0,2064	0,3863	0,0005
std.	20	0,0131	0,0111	0,0093	1,4206	0,0110	0,0323	0,0388	0,0343
23	400	0,0012	0,0035	0,0015	0,7467	0,0528	0,2520	0,3882	0,0006
std.	18	0,0146	0,0110	0,0093	1,4056	0,0101	0,0343	0,0388	0,0346
24	431	0,0015	0,0034	0,0014	0,6500	0,0534	0,1868	0,3879	0,0005
std.	22	0,0133	0,0110	0,0093	1,9356	0,0107	0,0348	0,0381	0,0325
25	430	0,0015	0,0033	0,0014	0,4000	0,0531	0,1903	0,3878	0,0006
std.	21	0,0133	0,0108	0,0093	0,8732	0,0112	0,0356	0,0384	0,0324
26	421	0,0014	0,0033	0,0013	0,5367	0,0532	0,2121	0,3898	0,0007

continued on next page

Table 4.6 — *continued from previous page*

state	Y_T	y	π_{price}	π_{wage}	$def.$	$vac.$	LSu	HSu	k
std.	19	0,0138	0,0108	0,0095	1,1163	0,0106	0,0321	0,0385	0,0368
27	430	0,0014	0,0034	0,0014	0,4433	0,0536	0,1914	0,3886	0,0009
std.	21	0,0128	0,0109	0,0098	0,9034	0,0107	0,0349	0,0398	0,0427
28	427	0,0014	0,0035	0,0015	0,4900	0,0533	0,1972	0,3876	0,0008
std.	21	0,0131	0,0110	0,0095	0,9342	0,0110	0,0338	0,0390	0,0372
29	430	0,0015	0,0035	0,0015	0,4667	0,0532	0,1903	0,3891	0,0006
std.	21	0,0123	0,0110	0,0096	1,0160	0,0102	0,0336	0,0389	0,0363
mean	427	0,0014	0,0034	0,0014	0,5061	0,0535	0,1973	0,3881	0,0007
	21	0,0129	0,0109	0,0095	1,0814	0,0107	0,0338	0,0388	0,0359

111

4. THE MODEL VS. STYLIZED FACTS

5
Concluding Remarks

"All models are wrong, but some are useful."
G. E. P. Box (1979)

In this book we present and agent-based computational model in which the macroeconomy is modelled as a "[...] *complex system where aggregate behaviour is determined by the complicated interaction among individuals operating in a simple way at the micro level*"(Kirman, 1999, p.5). In the model a large number of heterogeneous firms interact between them in markets for the Investment Goods, while firms and households interact in local markets for the Consumption Good and labour services. Other interactions take place between firms and banks in the credit market. All these trades are dispersed and randomly determined. Agents are bounded rational. They use simple, routinised strategies in order to update their choice variables, while selection mechanisms force unprofitable firms to exit the market.

Simulations of the model reveal that a fully decentralized economy, with no help from the Walrasian Auctioneer, is able to display regular behaviour on a macroeconomic scale. We *grow* an economy that replicates some interesting stylized facts both at the industrial dynamics level and at a macroeconomic scale. At the end, the message that this work would like to bring is methodological: agent-based techniques represent a practical and feasible approach of doing research in the world of complexity economics.

In the remainder of this Chapter, we shall discuss possible directions for future research. A first direction is the one consisting in extensions to the base model. As we have already mentioned, this work is part of a wider research project. Therefore, some extensions to the CATS model are already being implemented. Still, there remain open issues for further research. Some of the extensions would allow the model to replicate additional stylized facts, others would permit to inject to the model empirical evidence at a micro level. An interesting extension could be the introduction of the distance (in terms of costs), and as a further step, a more realistic geographical dimension. This may prove helpful in the study of the networks of firms - banks and the financial contagion and bankruptcy chain effects. Moreover, we could make use of genetic algorithms and more sophisticated learning processes.

Another promising direction is the validation and calibration of the model. Even though ABM and simulations have been extensively used in economics, only in the last few years researchers have started to consider the issue of validation, i.e. in other words, to check for the correctness of the model and its results. In Sargent's words, *"model validation is usually defined to mean substantiation that a computerized model within its domain of applicability possesses a satisfactory range of accuracy consistent with the intended application of the model"*(Sargent, 1998, p. 32). A first contribution to CATS model validation is given by Bianchi, Cirillo, Gallegati and Vagliasindi in Bianchi *et al.* (2007a) and Bianchi *et al.* (2007b).

This model, in-progress and future extensions (those mentioned above and others), aims to build an artificial economy from the bottom-up. That is, a "laboratory" able to describe how an economic system works. Moreover, this laboratory would allow, on the one hand, to conduct policy experiments (fiscal, monetary, and/or labour market policies), and on the other hand, the study of the relationships between the individual behaviour and the macroeconomic properties of a system.

Bibliography

AGHION, P. AND HOWITT, P. (1992). *A model of growth through creative destruction.* Econometrica, 60(2), pp. 323 – 351.

ANDERSON, P. W. (1995). *Physics: The opening to complexity.* PNAS, 92(15), pp. 6653–6654.

ARTHUR, W. B. (1999). *Complexity and the economy.* Science, 284(5411), pp. 107–109.

ARTHUR, W. B. (1994). *Increasing Return and Path Dependence in the Economy.* University of Michigan Press, Ann Arbor, MI.

ATTFIELD, C. AND SILVERSTONE, B. (1997). *Okun's coefficient: A comment.* Review of Economics and Statistics, 79, pp. 326–329.

AXTELL, R. L. (2001). *Zipf distribution of u.s. firm sizes.* Science, 293(5536), pp. 1818–1820.

BACKHOUSE, R. E. (2002). *The Penguin History of Economics.* Penguin Books, London.

BALMANN, A. (2000). *Modeling land use with multi-agent systems - perspectives for the analysis of agricultural policies.* Tech. rep.

BEINHOCKER, E. D. (2006). *The Origin of Wealth.* Harvard Business School Press, Boston, MA.

BERGER, T. (2001). *Agent-based spatial models applied to agriculture: a simulation tool for technology diffusion, resource use changes and policy analysis.* Agricultural Economics, 25(2-3), pp. 245–260.

BIANCHI, C., CIRILLO, P., GALLEGATI, M. AND VAGLIASINDI, P. A. (2007a). *Validating and calibrating agent-based models: A case study.* Computational Economics, 30(3), pp. 245–264.

BIANCHI, C., CIRILLO, P., GALLEGATI, M. AND VAGLIASINDI, P. A. (2007b). *Validation in agent-based models: An investigation on the cats model.* J. ECON. BEHAV. ORGAN., In Press, Corrected Proof.

BLANCHFLOWER, D. AND OSWALD, A. (1994). *The Wage Curve.* MIT Press, Cambridge, MA.

BOYD, I. L. (2007). *Zoology: a search for pattern in form and function.* Journal of Zoology, 271(1), pp. 1–2.

CARD, D. (1995). *The wage curve: A review.* Journal of Economic Literature, 33, pp. 785–799.

CARR, B. J. (2001). *Complexity in cosmology.* In *Phase Transitions in the Early Universe: Theory and Observations* (edited by DE VEGA, H. J., KHALATNIKOV, I. M. AND SANCHEZ, N. G.), vol. 40 of *NATO science series. Series II, Mathematics, Physics and Chemistry*, p. 267. Kluwer Academic Publishers, Boston, MA.

CASSIDY, J. (1996). *The decline of economics.* The New Yorker, pp. 50–60.

DELLI GATTI, D., DI GUILMI, C., GAFFEO, E., GIULIONI, G., GALLEGATI, M. AND PALESTRINI, A. (2005a). *A new approach to business fluctuations: heterogeneous interacting agents, scaling laws and financial fragility.* J. ECON. BEHAV. ORGAN., 56(4), pp. 489–512.

DELLI GATTI, D., GAFFEO, E., GALLEGATI, M. AND PALESTRINI, A. (2005b). *The apprentice wizard: monetary policy policy, complexity and learning.* New Mathematics and Natural Computation, 1(1), pp. 109–128.

DELLI GATTI, D., GALLEGATI, M., GIULIONI, G. AND PALESTRINI, A. (2003). *Financial fragility, patterns of firms' entry and exit and aggregate dynamics.* J. ECON. BEHAV. ORGAN., 51(1), pp. 79–97.

DOSI, G., FAGIOLO, G. AND ROVENTINI, A. (2005a). *Animal spirits, lumpy investment, and endogenous business cycles.* Lem working paper series, Laboratory of Economics and Management (LEM), Sant'Anna School of Advanced Studies, Pisa, Italy.

DOSI, G., FAGIOLO, G. AND ROVENTINI, A. (2005b). *An evolutionary model of endogenous business cycles.* Lem working paper series, Laboratory of Economics and Management (LEM), Sant'Anna School of Advanced Studies, Pisa, Italy.

DURLAUF, S. N. (2005). *Complexity and empirical economics.* The Economic Journal, 115(504), pp. F225–F243.

FAGIOLO, G., DOSI, G. AND GABRIELE, R. (2004a). *Matching, bargaining, and wage setting in an evolutionary model of labor market and output dynamics.* Advances in Complex Systems [A Multidisciplinary Quarterly Journal], Vol. 7(No. 2), pp. 157–186.

FAGIOLO, G., DOSI, G. AND GABRIELE, R. (2004b). *Towards an evolutionary interpretation of aggregate labour market regularities.* LEM Working Paper Series 02, Sant'Anna School for Advanced Studies.

FUJIWARA, Y., AOYAMA, H., DI GUILMI, C., SOUMA, W. AND GALLEGATI, M. (2004a). *Gibrat and pareto-zipf revisited with european firms.* Physica A: Statistical Mechanics and its Applications, 344(1-2), pp. 112–116.

117

FUJIWARA, Y., DI GUILMI, C., AOYAMA, H., GALLEGATI, M. AND SOUMA, W. (2004b). *Do pareto-zipf and gibrat laws hold true? an analysis with european firms.* Physica A: Statistical Mechanics and its Applications, 335(1-2), pp. 197–216.

GAFFEO, E., CATALANO, M., CLEMENTI, F., DELLI GATTI, D., GALLEGATI, M. AND RUSSO, A. (2007). *Reflections on modern macroeconomics: Can we travel along a safer road?* Physica A: Statistical Mechanics and its Applications, 382(1), pp. 89–97.

GAFFEO, E., GALLEGATI, M., GIULIONI, G. AND PALESTRINI, A. (2003). *Power laws and macroeconomic fluctuations.* Physica A: Statistical Mechanics and its Applications, 324(1-2), pp. 408–416.

GALLEGATI, M., DELLI GATTI, D., DI GUILMI, C. AND GIULIONI, G. (2003a). *Financial fragility, industrial dynamics and business fluctuations in an agent based model.* SSRN eLibrary.

GALLEGATI, M., GIULIONI, G. AND KICHIJI, N. (2003b). *Complex dynamics and financial fragility in an agent based model.* Computational Science.

GRAZIANI, A. (2003). *The Monetary Theory of Production.* Cambridge University Press, Cambridge.

GRIMM, V., REVILLA, E., BERGER, U., JELTSCH, F., MOOIJ, W. M., RAILSBACK, S. F., THULKE, H.-H., WEINER, J., WIEGAND, T. AND DEANGELIS, D. L. (2005). *Pattern-oriented modeling of agent-based complex systems: Lessons from ecology.* Science, 310(5750), pp. 987–991.

GUMMESSON, E. (2006). *Qualitative research in management: addressing complexity, context and persona.* Management Decision, 44(2), pp. 167–179.

HAHN, F. (1982). *Money and Inflation.* Blackwell Publishing, Oxford.

118

HOPENHAYN, H. A. (1992). *Entry, exit, and firm dynamics in long run equilibrium.* Econometrica, 60(5), pp. 1127–1150.

INGRAO, B. AND ISRAEL, G. (1990). *The Invisible Hand.* MIT Press, Cambridge, MA.

KEYNES, J. M. (1923). *A Tract on Monetary Reform*, vol. IV of *The Collected Writings of John Maynard Keynes.* Palgrave MacMillian.

KIRMAN, A. P. (1999). *Beyond the rapresentative agent*, chap. Interaction and Markets, pp. 1–44. Edward Elgar, Cheltenham.

KIRMAN, A. P. (1992). *Whom or what does the representative individual represent?* Journal of Economic Perspectives, 6(2), pp. 117–36.

KOCH, C. AND LAURENT, G. (1999). *Complexity and the nervous system.* Science, 284(5411), pp. 96–98.

LEIJONHUFVUD, A. (1996). *Towards a not-too-rational macroeconomics.* Colander (1996), pp. 39–55.

LU, H. AND SHI, Y. (2007). *Complexity of public transport networks.* Tsinghua Science & Technology, 12(2), pp. 204–213.

MALANSON, G. P., ZENG, Y. AND WALSH, S. J. (2006). *Landscape frontiers, geography frontiers: Lessons to be learned.* The Professional Geographer, 58(4), pp. 383–396.

MARTIN, R. AND SUNLEY, P. (2007). *Complexity thinking and evolutionary economic geography.* Journal of Economic Geography, p. lbm019.

MAS-COLELL, A., WHINSTON, M. D. AND GREEN, J. R. (1995). *Microeconomic Theory.* Oxford University Press, New York.

MILLER, J. H. AND PAGE, S. E. (2007). *Complex Adaptive Systems. An Introduction to Computational Models of Social Life.* Princeton University Press.

119

MIROVSKI, P. (1989). *More Heat than Light: Economics as Social Physics, Physics as Nature's Economics.* Cambridge University Press.

PARKER, D. C., MANSON, S. M., JANSSEN, M. A., HOFFMANN, M. J. AND DEADMAN, P. (2003). *Multi-agent systems for the simulation of land-use and land-cover change: A review.* Annals of the Association of American Geographers, 93(2), pp. 314–337.

PARRISH, J. K. AND EDELSTEIN-KESHET, L. (1999). *Complexity, pattern, and evolutionary trade-offs in animal aggregation.* Science, 284(5411), pp. 99–101.

PAVARD, B. AND DUGDALE, J. (2000). *The contribution of complexity theory to the study of socio-technical cooperative systems.* InterJournal Complex Systems.

PEARCE, N. AND MERLETTI, F. (2006). *Complexity, simplicity, and epidemiology.* Int. J. Epidemiol., 35(3), pp. 515–519.

PHILLIPS, A. W. (1958). *The relation between unemployment and the rate of change of money wages in united kingdom, 1861-1957.* Economica.

PISSARIDES, C. A. (2000). *Equilibrium Unemployment Theory.* MIT Press, Cambridge, MA, 2nd ed.

PRACHOWNY, M. (1993). *Okun's law: Theoretical foundations and revised estimates.* Review of Economics and Statistics, 75, pp. 331–336.

RIND, D. (1999). *Complexity and climate.* Science, 284(5411), pp. 105–107.

RUSSO, A., CATALANO, M., GAFFEO, E., GALLEGATI, M. AND NAPOLETANO, M. (2007). *Industrial dynamics, fiscal policy and r&d: Evidence from a computational experiment.* J. ECON. BEHAV. ORGAN., 64(3-4), pp. 426–447.

SARGENT, T. J. (1998). *Verification and validation in simulation models*. In *Proceedings of 1998 Winter Simulation Conference*, pp. 52–64.

SMITH, A. (1776). *An Inquiry into the Nature and Causes of the Wealth of Nations*. Fifth edition (1789) ed. Republished from: Edwin Cannan's annotated edition, 1904, Methuen & Co., Ltd.

SMITH, D. E. AND FOLEY, D. K. (2002). *Is utility theory so different from thermodynamics?* Santa Fe Institute Working Paper, (02-04-016).

SOLOW, R. M. (1956). *A contribution to the theory of economic growth*. Quarterly Journal of Economics, 70(1), pp. 65–94.

STANLEY, H. E., AMARAL, L. A. N., BULDYREV, S. V., GOPIKRISHNAN, P., PLEROU, V. AND SALINGER, M. A. (2002). *Self-organized complexity in economics and finance*. PNAS, 99(90001), pp. 2561–2565.

STANLEY, M., AMARAL, L. A. N., BULDYREV, S. V., HAVLING, S., LESHORN, H., MAAS, P., SALINGER, M. A. AND STANLEY, H. E. (1996). *Scaling behaviour in the growth of companies*. Nature, 379, pp. 804–806.

STEWART, I. (1989). *Does God Play Dice? The Mathematics of Chaos*. Basic Blackwell, Cambridge, MA.

STIGLITZ, J. (1989). *Imperfect information in the product market*. North-Holland, Amsterdam.

STRAND, R., RORTVEIT, G. AND SCHEI, E. (2005). *Complex systems and human complexity in medicine*. Complexus, 2, pp. 2–6.

SYLOS LABINI, F. AND PIETRONERO, L. (2001). *Complexity in cosmology*. ArXiv Astrophysics e-prints.

TESFATSION, L. (2002). *Agent-based computational economics: Growing economies from the bottom up.* Artif. Life, 8(1), pp. 55–82.

TESFATSION, L. (2003). *Agent-based computational economics: modeling economies as complex adaptive systems.* Information Sciences, 149(4), pp. 262–268.

TESFATSION, L. (2005). *Agent-based computational laboratories for the experimental study of complex economic systems.* Computing in Economics and Finance 2005 72, Society for Computational Economics.

TROISI, A., WONG, V. AND RATNER, M. A. (2005). *From the cover: An agent-based approach for modeling molecular self-organization.* PNAS, 102(2), pp. 255–260.

WALDROP, M. M. (1992). *Complexity: The Emerging Science at the Edge of Order and Chaos.* Tochstone, New York.

WENG, G., BHALLA, U. S. AND IYENGAR, R. (1999). *Complexity in biological signaling systems.* Science, 284(5411), pp. 92–96.

WERNER, B. T. (1999). *Complexity in natural landform patterns.* Science, 284(5411), pp. 102–104.

WHITESIDES, G. M. AND ISMAGILOV, R. F. (1999). *Complexity in chemistry.* Science, 284(5411), pp. 89–92.

WINDRUM, P. (2004). *Neo-schumpeterian simulation models.* Research Memoranda 002, Maastricht Economic Research Institute on Innovation and Technology - MERIT.

WINTER, S. G., KANIOVSKI, Y. M. AND DOSI, G. (2003). *A baseline model of industry evolution.* Journal of Evolutionary Economics, 13(4), pp. 355–383.

Index

Ideas

maybe spatial characteristics
different laws + environment in
different places.

Made in the USA
Lexington, KY
05 July 2016